Woman Traveler

To Susan Bailey   *April 25, 1992*

Woman Traveler:
How to get over the economic
hurdles along the way

Carry it on !

Blanche Fitzpatrick

Blanche Fitzpatrick

Pemberton Publishers   Boston, MA.

Library of Congress Cataloging in Publication Data

Fitzpatrick, Blanche
Woman Traveler

1. Woman's economic role in the United States
2. Woman as producer 3. Woman as re-producer
4.. Woman as consumer 5. Woman and "the system"   I. Title

LC. 90-91894
ISBN 0-9627397-1-5

Pemberton Publishers
P.O. Box 441558
Somerville,MA 02144
(617) 868-6065

I saw her upon nearer view
  A spirit, yet a woman too!
. . .
A being breathing thoughtful breath
  A traveler between life and death.

William Wordsworth

Acknowledgments

In addition to acknowledgments in the text for permission to reproduce cartoons which illuminate the text, and to the footnoted sources of data drawn from other publications, I would like to express appreciation to:

Reference librarians in many libraries who have invariably been helpful and generous with their time and expertise, especially at the Boston Public Library, Government Documents section; Cambridge Public Library; Mugar Library at Boston University; Widener Library and Schlesinger Library at Harvard University; and the University of California at La Jolla; Chris Barrington, for typing the manuscript initially; and, not least, the helpful specialists at the Office for Information Technology at Harvard.

CONTENTS

Tables and Charts

Chapter I

OVERVIEW - ECONOMIC SURVIVAL:

A Woman's Lifetime Experience

cathy®   **by Cathy Guisewite**

If you were planning to drive across the United States, I could tell you a few things--I've driven it a number of times. If you're leaving Boston for Los Angeles, or going from San Francisco to Jacksonville, I could suggest a few places where drivers sometimes have problems. I wouldn't list the scenic wonders--most people already know about Grand Canyon and Yosemite. But if I cared about your safety, and wanted to help you have a smooth trip, I might say, "Last year, snow blocked the Donner Pass in April;" or "You may need extra water when you're crossing the Bonneville Salt Flats;"or "Plan to hit the Chicago area before 4:00 p.m." These directions wouldn't be perfect, because by the time you start out, the snows may have melted, and new highways may have been built. But it helps to know what to watch out for--some things don't change much.

If you're now in your teens or twenties, you may now and then be thinking about where you're going with your life. Friends your own age don't know the routes either, and you may have few friends over thirty who might be able to report on the bumps along their way. So this book is intended to give you a few clues as to what your choices are, and what penalties you are likely to encounter as a woman. This book does not presume to tell you how to get along with your parents, teachers, or friends of either sex. As one disgusted teenager told me, "We can figure those things out

for ourselves--what we need to know about is jobs, and
money!" This book deals with economic survival. Once you're
on your own, how are you going to pay the rent, or make the
mortgage payments; provide food and clothing for yourself
(and your children, if any); pay for a car and have a little
fun as you go along?

Economic survival depends, first and foremost, on the
income you receive from your job. Even a pinchpenny has to
have some funds to work with, so a lot is riding on your
choice of a job. Practically everyone has to work for a
living, and the job choices we make will set the weekly
amounts we get. So the first topic this book will consider
is: <u>Woman as Producer</u>. For at least the last thirty years,
according to government statistics, the <u>average annual
earnings of women who work full-time, full-year, have been
about two-thirds of the earnings of fully-employed men.</u> In
1986, women high school graduates (with no college) had lower
median income than fully-employed men with only an 8th grade
education--$15,947 for the women, and $18,541 for the men.
Women with 4 years of college had lower income than men high
school graduates--$22,412 for the women, $24,701 for the men[1]

Does this prove that employers discriminate against
women? There is documented evidence from many suits filed
over the past twenty or thirty years that sex discrimination
has been practiced by some employers. Millions of dollars of
back pay have been awarded women as a result of suits by the
United States Department of Labor, the Equal Employment
Opportunity Commission, or by individual women. Employers
have been found to discriminate against women by refusing to
hire or promote women for certain jobs, by paying men more
for essentially the same job, or by giving similar jobs
different titles. Discriminating employers have included
A.T. & T., Wendy's, prestigious law firms and academic
institutions.

But there is another explanation for the lower average
wages of women relative to men -- that is, the different
kinds of jobs usually held by each sex. So a major area to
look into is the question of job choice. Why do women take
the kinds of jobs they do? That is, why does each new crop
of women coming out of high school or college choose to
produce goods and services that have a low dollar value to
society, which is expressed in low weekly pay rates?

For some women, job choices are explained by necessity.
A substantial number of high school women will not graduate
because of pregnancy. (The United States has the highest
rate of teen pregnancy in the world.)[2] The resulting lack of
a high school diploma, added to child care problems, may
limit the job options for years to come, even for a lifetime.
But even women with high school, or college, or professional

degrees often "choose" jobs which are low-pay and dead-end. To help explain women's job choices, in Chapter Two we will consider a number of areas: whether the formal and informal education system (parents, schools, TV, movies, magazines) influences women to attend less prestigious schools, to prepare for stereotyped "Women's jobs"; whether women are as likely as men to be admitted to top-level education and training programs after high school; whether women are physically and mentally capable of performing "men's jobs"; whether home tasks limit women's aspirations and achievement in the paid labor force.

Another factor affecting women's economic survival is related to the first. Women not only produce some of the goods and services that we all consume--women also have the major role as producers of the next generation, the children who will become the workers, executives, scholars, military and government officials of the future. Although this role is of the utmost importance to the United States (and globally), and is so celebrated in song and story, in terms of financial returns, motherhood is a very poorly-rewarded occupation. (You don't go into it for the money, right?) But although money is not the only goal of life, it is much like breathing. Breathing is not the most fun thing you do all day, but without it, staying alive is a lot harder.

Women often must anticipate the problems of caring for children. Jobs offering hours that are convenient for mothers with school-age children often pay less (for example, retail sales) and part-time work in any job is pretty sure to bring in a smaller pay check. Full-time jobs require child care arrangements; good, reliable, conveniently-located child care is often expensive, and usually hard to find. After child care expenses are deducted, the woman worker's low weekly income shrinks still further.

Moreover, money (profit) matters to employers also, and this may reduce women's job options. It is understandable that a profit-seeking businessman prefers that workers be as productive as possible. A kind-hearted employer who permits frequent absences by employees when child-care arrangements break down, or when a child is ill, may find that a more hard-hearted employer can undercut him in price. Thus working mothers may be more subject to layoffs and unemployment.

For mothers forced to turn to public welfare programs, income is even more limited. The level of benefits to "welfare mothers" in Massachusetts is so low that there has been a continuing campaign to raise the level of assistance UP to the poverty level (and in other states, the situation is as bad or worse). Whatever her income source, the presence of children is likely to affect the woman's balance

sheet, of income and outgo. So in Chapter Three we will look
at woman's role as <u>Re-producer</u>, and its effect on her
economic survival in youth, middle age and old age.

Economic survival is affected by spending as well as
by income. In Chapter Four we will look at <u>Woman as Consumer</u>.
If women, in addition to earning lower hourly pay, and/or
working reduced hours because of child care problems, are
required to pay higher prices, or to consume unnecessary
items, their general purchasing power, and their standard of
living, would be still further eroded. Is this a far-fetched
notion, or is there any evidence that women are also
disadvantaged as consumers ? In a truly competitive market,
we might conceive it to be impossible; but some markets are
less competitive than others.For example, women are much more
likely than men to undergo surgical procedures - almost twice
as many were performed on women in 1985, as compared to men[3].
.Also, studies repeatedly indicate that women purchase and
use more prescription drugs than men do.[4] On insurance,
females seeking individual coverage are routinely charged
higher prices for individual disability or health insurance
than would be charged to a comparable male.

The lack of access to credit also restricts women's
options as consumers. Despite federal and many state laws
requiring lenders to provide credit without discrimination
based on sex, (or other characteristics), the typical low-
paid woman will have greater difficulty in obtaining loans
than will the typical higher-paid man. Thus more women than
men will be foreclosed from major consumption expenditures
(home ownership, new car), or from starting up a small
business.

Many of the above economic penalties incurred by women
are related to laws which were reviewed, passed, or rejected,
by predominantly male legislatures. So in Chapter Five we
will look at <u>Women and "the System</u>," as another key to the
low economic status of the female half of the population.
Enforcement of laws or executive orders is carried on, or
ignored, by cabinet members, or agency heads, who are
predominantly male. Decisions on women's rights under
federal and state laws are made by a predominantly male
judiciary. Not until 1981 was a woman named to the nine-
member United States Supreme Court. Woman's minority
presence in the political and judicial systems affects her
economic status in ways ranging from unequal access to
education and training, exclusion from top-level military and
civil service jobs, to adverse treatment under laws and in
the Social Security system. Women parents without male
partners increasingly face economic disaster, according to
the 1983 report of the U.S. Commission on Civil Rights.[5]

For women especially, economic insecurity tends to worsen with age. A woman's lifetime may be somewhat longer than that of a man born in the same year--and may SEEM much longer, for an elderly woman often ill as well as poverty-stricken. Of all the elderly receiving Supplementary Security Income (means-tested federal old age assistance), three-quarters were women in 1986.[6] . The fact that the poor elderly are predominantly women is not surprising, since a woman's lifetime of low-paid jobs and intermittent employment is reflected in low monthly benefits under Social Security. Likewise, a smaller percentage of women than men receive any private pension, and their benefits on average are smaller, because of women's usual low-wage employment pattern.[7] Chapter VI reviews the ways in which women may cope with economic problems encountered over a lifetime.

At this point, you may well ask--since there are many identifiable groups in the American economy who suffer severe economic penalties--blacks, Hispanics, Asians--why focus on women only? One answer: to address the lifetime economic penalties suffered by women is to address the problems of half the population, of EVERY racial and ethnic group.

So this rather small book will try to provide a map of the likely deserts, mountains, and road washouts you are likely to encounter as you make your way from age 15 to age 75. Roads and circumstances change, or course, though not so spectacularly as is sometimes reported. If you believe that the "affirmative action" programs of the 1960's and 1970's have brought equal economic status for all women, think again. As pointed out above, and shown for at least the last thirty years in government statistics, full-time, full-year women workers have persistently earned about two thirds as much as their male counterparts. About 2000 years ago, the Bible reported the ransom for males as 50 shekels, and for females, 30 shekels. (That's about two-thirds).[8] Pretty slow going.

Much of the material included in this book comes from a course "Women in the Economy" which I have taught at Boston University for about ten years.

So--before you go down that lonesome road--take a look at the map.

---

[1]U.S. Department of Labor, Women's Bureau, Time of Change: 1983 Handbook on Women Workers , Bulle ti n 298 (Washington, D>C>: U.S. Government Printing Office, 1983, Table III-1, p.82. (Hereafter cited as 1983 Handbook) U.S. Department of Commerce, Bureau of the Census, "Money Income of Households, Families and Persons in the United States: 1986", Current Population Reports, Series P-60, No. 159 (Washington, D.C.: U.S. Government Printing Office, 1986) T.27, pp.l00-0l (Hereafter cited as CPR, P-60, No.l59).

[2]Nadine Brozan, "U.S. Leads Industrialized Nations in Teen Age Births and Abortions", New York Times. 3/l3/85, p.A 1.

[3] U.S. Department of Commerce, Bureau of Census, Statistical Abstract of the United States, 1988. (Washington, D.C.: U.S. Government Printing Office) Table 157, p.l00. (Hereafter cited as 1988 Statistical Abstract)

[4] L.M. Verbrugge and R.P.Steiner, "Prescribing Drugs to Men and Women", Health Psychology 1985, 4 (1) pp.79-98.

[5] U.S. Commission on Civil Rights. A Growing Crisis: Disadvantaged Women and their Children (releaased 4/11/83)

[6] U.S. Department of Health and Human Services, Social Security Bulletin . (Washington, D.C.: U.S. Government Printing Office , 1987). May l987, p.20. (Hereafter cited as Social Security Bulletin.)

[7] Statistical Abstract. 1988. T.568, p.344.

[8] The Bible, Leviticus, Chapter 27.

Chapter II

WOMEN EARNING MONEY (BUT NOT MUCH)

THE PROBLEM: Generally speaking, women who WORK FULL TIME,
                FULL YEAR earn about two-thirds as much as men
                who work full time, full year. (In 1955, it
                was 64%; in 1973, it was 57%; in 1986, it was
                64%.)[1]

                It doesn't stop with the small pay check.
                Because women earn low pay, or may stop
                working temporarily when their children are
                small, their unemployment compensation will
                average less than for men, or they may be
                denied benefits by state rules.

                Because women earn low pay, or may stop
                working temporarily when their children are
                small, Social Security benefits on their own
                account will average less than those for men
                at retirement., and they are likely to receive
                smaller private pensions, or none at all.

-- -- -- -- -- -- -- -- -- -- -- -- -- -- -- -- -- -- -- --

Of course, some women are right up there with the big
bucks--Cyndi Lauper, Diana Ross, Bette Midler, Connie Chung,
Cher--but most are in the lower income brackets. This means
that while John may buy a condo, Jane may have to settle for
a 3rd floor walkup; for a Chevy instead of a Volvo; for T.J.
Maxx instead of Ralph Lauren. Even harder to take if Jane is
bringing up children as a single parent--and millions of

women are in that situation today--she may be unable to earn
enough to provide them with the basic necessities--enough of
the right food, a decent home, presentable clothing. A
prostitute interviewed recently by the Boston Globe pointed
out; "I got two kids. I tried working at Bradlees. I tried
work at Zayre. I need the money."[2] Such jobs in retail sales
paid about $5.37 an hour in 1986.[3]

AND if Jane should be laid off from her job in retail
sales, or factory, or restaurant, she will get lower
Unemployment Compensation than John, because of that lower
pay. ((On an annual basis, in 1982 the average Unemployment
Compensation benefit for women was below the poverty line for
a single person, while the average for men was above the
poverty line for two persons.)[4] AND Jane will receive even
less Unemployment Compensation if she "chooses" to work part-
time in order to care for her children; she may in fact not
be eligible for Unemployment Compensation unless she is
willing to accept full-time work if offered, regardless of
her children's ages, or if she has "chosen" to work as a
"Temp" in order to fit in with her husband's work schedule,
or other family needs.. Like part-time work, temporary
workers are mainly a benefit to the employer, who avoids the
cost of providing fringe benefits of health insurance,
vacation pay, and pension contributions. Choosing "Home
work" to solve the problem of non-existent child care
options, has even worse effects on income, because employers
often evade paying employment taxes completely.and ignore
minimum wage or other laws affecting worker health and
safety. (To find out about illegal work-at-home schemes,
write: Social Security Administration, Division of Public
Inquiries, 6401 Security Blvd., Baltimore, MD 21235.)

AND when Jane is old and grey, her Social Security
benefits will be substantially less than John's because of a
lifetime spent working at low-paid jobs, and possibly part-
time work, with periods out of the work force while raising a
family. (The average Social Security benefit for women 65
and older, on their own account was $371 per month in 1983;
for men the average was $478 per month.[5] YES, all you young
guys, Social Security is a long way off--like around the
corner.

"ARE WE HAVING FUN YET?" asks Zippy. Then how about a
few more chuckles . Women are less likely to have adequate
private pensions to supplement Social Security benefits,
because the places where women are concentrated (small
retail, food service, or manufacturing firms) are less
likely to provide such fringe benefits. Because some women
are more likely than men to live to a very old age, (there
are twice as many women as men age 75 and older)[6] Jane will
possibly have a very long time to wish she had gone into some
more financially-rewarding employment.

Look at Table 2-1 on the next page. The occupations where women are in the majority (secretary, clerical and health fields) are at the low end of dollar earnings for both sexes. Professional occupations where women are the majority of workers (teacher, registered nurse) tend to be less well paid than the professions (doctor, lawyer) where men predominate. Trade and technical fields where women are the majority of workers (hairdresser, dental assistant) pay less than the skilled trades which are almost exclusively male (machinist, electrician). (Other tables in Appendix A reinforce this pattern.)

. When specific occupations, such as accountant, are further broken down by job duties, women are concentrated in the lower-paid classes. (Appendix Table A-1)

In government employment, also, when ranked by job classification, women are scarce at the top. (Appendix Table A-2)

Talk about coming a long, long way baby! Say, have you noticed how far there is to go.

So, that's the problem. Women in general occupy the lower-rated jobs, and thus are more likely than men to earn lower wages; to collect lower Unemployment Compensation, or be denied any unemployment compensation at all; and to receive lower Social Security benefits, or private pensions, in their old age.

What we want to do in this chapter is to understand two things:
1   Why men and women are unequally represented in "good" jobs.
2.   What you can do about it, to give yourself a better chance at economic survival.

*   *   *   *   *   *   *   *

Why are women the majority of workers in low paid jobs, and men the majority among high-paid workers? John is more likely to be a doctor, machinist, or truck driver, while Jane is more likely to be a teacher, stitcher, or secretary. Let's eliminate a few of the usual explanations right off the bat.

Are girls and women less intelligent than boys and Men? NO, NO, NO.

If you think so, you've been brain-washed by Dennis-the-Menace, mother-in-law jokes, TV comedies, and ads showing women leaping for joy after using a new floor wax. Actually, study after study has shown that girls on average do better than boys in school grades from kindergarten through college, even in high school math. Fewer girls take advanced math courses in high school, it should be noted, possibly reflecting family and faculty pressure on boys to take math NO MATTER WHAT. Boys' better performance on Mathematics and Science sections of SAT's reflects the higher percentage of boys taking four or more years of these courses in high school (61% of boys, 52% of girls). A 1987 study by American College Testing showed a very strong correlation between the number of years of Math and Science courses, and the average scores on these tests.[7]

A recent study of 8th graders in 20 countries found that "Overall, both sexes did equally well in arithmetic, algebra, and statistics."[8] Peer pressure, as well as the normal doubts of both boys and girls, as to what is the "right" thing to do in any situation, contributes to the smaller percentage of girls in high school courses in math and the physical sciences. As one mother reported:

> "Not everything has changed. My daughter, in the seventh grade, won a math contest. In the eighth grade, another contest was held, but I found the contest form on her desk and asked her why she hadn't sent it in. She started to cry and said "I'm afraid I'll win.' She had been getting pressure from the boys."[9]

Critics have pointed out that standardized tests typically refer to males and male experiences twice as often as they refer to females and female experiences. (A federal judge in New York recently ruled that the awarding of state merit scholarships on the basis of scores in Scholastic Aptitude Tests discriminates against girls and violates the equal protection clause of the Federal Constitution. Until a few years ago, boys usually scored higher on the Quantitative sections of the S.A.T., and girls higher on the Verbal section. Then the test was changed, allegedly to "create a better balance for the scores between the sexes";as a result of the change, boys now average higher scores on both sections of the test. We may well ask -- who's asking the right questions?

Both New York and Massachusetts have based their awards of public scholarships on the S.A.T. scores. National Merit Scholarships have employed the Preliminary S.A.T., taken in high school junior year, in making awards.)[10]

Table 2-1   11

Median Weekly Earnings: 1988 Annual Averages
Selected Occupations - White collar; blue collar;
technical and trade; professional.

Median weekly earnings of wage and salary workers who usually work full time, by detailed (3-digit census code) occupation and sex, 1988 annual averages.

Occupation	Both sexes Number of workers	Median Weekly Earnings Men	Women	Women as percent of total employed
Secretary	3,206,000	$ -	$ 312	99 %
Typist	603,000	-	298	94
Bookkeepers, accounting and auditing clerks	1,322,000	385	304	91
Computer Operator	754,000	414	312	66
Cashiers	936,000	222	185	79
Sales workers - retail and personal services	2,683,000	315	199	59
Textile sewing machine operators	669,000	216	191	89
Assemblers	1,025,000	349	251	45
Janitors and cleaners	1,397,000	272	213	22
Metal- and plastic-machine operators	438,000	403	302	18
Printing machine operators	301,000	395	-	14
Dental Assistants	104,000	-	267	98
Licensed Practical Nurse	299,000	-	336	94
Hairdressers and cosmetologists	268,000	-	229	90
Clinical laboratory technologists and technicians	216,000	484	399	74
Electrical and electronic equipment repairers	613,000	512	421	9
Machinists	456,000	440	-	5
Electricians	606,000	479	-	1
Teacher:				
Kindergarten and pre-kindergarten	253,000	-	320	97
Elementary school	1,264,000	522	476	84
Secondary school	1,064,000	580	491	49
Registered nurse	1,075,000	561	515	93
Social workers	458,000	434	420	64
Editors and reporters	198,000	588	412	47
Computer system analyst and scientist	421,000	730	594	30
Lawyer	366,000	930	774	26
Physician	254,000	815	572	25
Engineer	1,719,000	734	639	7

* NOTE: Weekly earnings do not include earnings from self-employment.

Medians and percents are not shown where the base is under 50,000. Such cases are indicated by dashes.

SOURCE: U.S. Department of Labor, Bureau of Labor Statistics, Current Population Survey. 1988 annual averages. (unpublished data)

<u>Are girls and women physical weaklings compared to boys and men?</u> NO, NO, NO.

The first all-woman crew flew an Air Force transport across the Atlantic in 1983.[11] Susan Butcher recemtly won the Alaskan Iditarod, a thousand-mile sled dog race, over ice and snow, through blizzards and whiteouts,for the fourth time.[12] Lynne Cox was the first (and so far the only) person to swim a 2.7 mile stretch of frigid water across the Bering Strait between Alaska and the Soviet island of Big Diomede. (She did it on a breakfast of a bagel and apple juice; and had been eating a lot of pasta and peanut butter.)[13]

On the average, men tend to have greater strength, while women have greater endurance, and therefore many records for extra-long distance running, or swims, are held by women. In any event, as machinery grows more sophisticated, push button skills have replaced physical strength as the requirement on most jobs.

BUT, if women ARE physically and mentally capable of holding the more demanding and better-paid jobs, why are they concentrated in low-paid jobs? Oversimplified, the answer is; <u>The fish don't see the water</u>--it's the way things are! Young girls (and boys) accept the world they find, and tend to follow their mothers and older sisters (or fathers and older brothers) along the traditional paths. Some girls are becoming more aware that they too can aim for the top--but it is still true that lower-income girls are less likely than their brothers to be encouraged by parents, teachers, and the education system in general to explore a wide range of future occupations and to prepare themselves for a lifetime of work by choosing top level colleges or vocational training programs.[14]

Half a century ago, Virginia Woolf wrote an essay "Three Guineas", discussing "Arthur's Education Fund", the practice by financially-pressed families of setting aside money for son's education, rather than daughters.During the recession of the early nineteen-eighties, when family financial pressures were affecting college applications, the admissions director of Williams College commented; "People are saying 'Put the money on the male'[15] ". When families cannot easily provide tuition funds, it is likely to be the son rather than the daughter who is encouraged to apply.

For most young women, it's easier to take a job right out of high school. A week's pay, even from a low-level clerical or factory job or McDonald's looks good when you're a teenager, and have never earned more than a few dollars as a baby-sitter. So you grab that job, and blow your paycheck at the Mall, on the latest clothes and records, and the big, gooey ice cream sundaes you've always yearned for. But even if once in a while you turn off the Madonna or Springsteen records, and try to figure out what you should do with your life, it's very hard for a teenager to cope with the educational system.

Does the educational system keep girls and women out of training and education for higher paid jobs?

Some years back, a Massachusetts teenager sent a letter to the Massachusetts State House, addressed "To Whom It May Concern." Her message: "I am being held back because I am a girl." Because her family owned a garage, she was interested in studying Auto Mechanics; she had applied to a public regional vocational-technical school but was denied admission because of her sex.[16] In other vocational schools, investigators for the U. S. General Accounting Office found that girls were discouraged from signing up for shop courses; the girls told investigators that they were "not allowed in the boys' building," The school administrator told the G.A.O. investigator that the girls had a mistaken impression.[17] (Actually, it's pretty easy to scare off kids who worry that almost everything they do is wrong--or, even worse, dumb.) As a result of such formal or informal discouragement, girls continue to be the majority of enrollment in Clerical and Health programs, preparing for low-paid jobs, while boys predominate in training for the better-paid Trade and Technical occupations, in carpentry, mechanical, or electrical skills.

When Alice de Rivera, as a teenager in 1969 sought admission to the Science High School in New York City, she found that girls were not admitted.[18] The University of Virginia was cited in 1964 at Congressional hearings on discrimination against women for having rejected applications from "21,000 women but not 1 man."[19]

Such clear-cut cases of sex discrimination in admission to academic or vocational institutions are now forbidden by federal law (1972 Title IX; 1988 Civil Rights Restoration Act) and by laws in many states as well. But the attitudes of some adults who operate the educational system are slow to change. Your parents, as well as many of today's teachers, school superintendents, and public officials and college administrators, grew up in a world where it was believed women didn't need as much education; husbands would provide the income while wives stayed home and cared for the children, and the home, did the laundry and prepared the meals. Today, however, most mothers are in the labor force, and many are restricted by limited education and training to the less desirable, low-paid, dead end jobs.

The vocational school faculty who favor the admission of boys over girls are likely to be "good guys" who see the world as it was in their youth. Carpenters, plumbers, auto mechanics have almost always worked in a rough "men only" world ; to let women in could threaten that world, especially with respect to wage levels. As a U. S. Department of Labor economist pointed out:

> "The chances of an occupation (having high earnings for men) are greatly decreased as the proportion of female workers increases.... Men in occupations dominated by women, while earning more than the women, are likely to earn less than men in other occupations."[20]

For evidence, look at Table 2-1 and Tables A-1 and A-2 in Appendix A .

It isn't only the skilled trades which discourage women entrants. Admission officials at colleges and universities, like their counterparts at public vocational schools, seem to share the attitude: "Keep out the ribbon clerks." Just the possibility that women may become the majority in a given profession is enough to cause the occupation to lose points in prestige ranking. In one study, students were asked to rate the prestige of several high-status professions (architect, professor, lawyer, physician, scientist); ratings of occupational prestige decreased when study group members were informed that women would become a higher percentage of the profession in the future.[21]

Twenty years ago, a professor at a woman's college in Connecticut asked students to evaluate a collection of articles in the fields of law, city planning, nutrition, and other specialized areas. The articles were bound into two sets. In one set a particular article would be identified as written by John McKay; in the other set, the same article would be identified as written by Joan McKay. . When the class of women students was asked to rate the articles on style and content, the writing attributed to male authors scored significantly higher.[22] That was in 1968. In 1982 researchers repeated the experiment at a co-educational institution, expanding authors' names to John, Joan, and J.T. This time, both men and women preferred the articles by John, followed by J.T., with Joan coming in third.[23] What's in a name? A name apparently is a package carrying the (unconscious) attitudes planted in our minds as we grow up.

If too many women are admitted to a particular university, male administrators,faculty and alumni fear that its prestige will be diminished.. Harvard Medical did not admit women students until 1946. Social perceptions change about as fast as the raindrops wear away Grand Canyon. The gate-keepers to colleges as well as to apprenticeships, who control access to better-paid fields, concentrate recruitment efforts on young men rather than young women, as a way of protecting their own income and prestige. But that's not the whole story.

The other possibility is: Are you holding yourself back?

Girls and women unconsciously absorb the message--from "Dick and Jane"-type readers and high school history texts, from "Moonlighting" on TV, from advertisements, from magazines, from movies, that they are not strong enough, or bright enough, or will "lose their femininity" if they prepare themselves for better-paid employment. So they just don't apply for apprenticeships, or to public vocational trade programs, or to the top academic institutions. The message persists, in spite of all the hoop-la about women's progress.

In fact, when high school girls were asked their job preferences in a Department of Labor survey in 1968, NINE jobs accounted for two-thirds of the girls' choices: secretary, teacher, (3 levels) office/clerical, professional nurse, hairdresser, sales clerk, social worker.[24] More recent studies confirm that when questioned as to job preference these low-paid occupations continue to top the lists for girls, while more boys choose to become engineers, lawyers, skilled workers or to enter other better-paid fields. There appears to be a very close relationship between the percentage of older women already in a particular occupation, and the percentage of new female entrants into that occupation.[25]

Recently when young boys and girls were asked: "If you woke up tomorrow and discovered that you were a (boy) (girl), how would your life be different?"
A girl answered, "I want to be an interior decorator, but if I were a boy I'd be an architect.
A boy answered, "If I were a girl, everybody would be better than me, because boys are better than girls."[26]

*   *   *   *   *   *   *   *

How you can cope: getting the most out of the educational system.

Look around you.

Listen to a 27 year old woman interviewed by the Boston Globe. "She can tell you how seven years of steady employment as a secretary, receptionist and clerk in the Boston economy has taught her the difference between earning a wage and making a living.

'When I graduated from high school I knew I didn't
'want to become a welfare mother, and I knew I had
the skills not to be one. But no matter how high
you go in clerical work, you're still at the ·
bottom...I set out a budget each month, but I take
home so little that I am always scraping...It gets
so terrible sometimes that I just sit down and
pray.'
She cannot afford necessary dental work for her older
son, or day care for her younger one. She cannot afford a
telephone".[27]

YOU HAVE A LIFETIME OF WORK AHEAD OF YOU. If you marry,
and have children, husbands may die, desert, divorce, become
ill or unemployed. Millions of young women in the U. S.
today are bringing up children alone, often because ex-
husbands and fathers skip out on responsibilities. Even in a
marriage which celebrates its Golden Wedding anniversary,
there are likely to be times when the male partner cannot
provide adequate family support because of illness,
unemployment, or simply because of his low earning power.

To give yourself and your children a chance for a
decent living standard, prepare yourself to use your highest
skills, in work which is satisfying and well-paid. While you
are still in high school, sample the Shop courses--carpentry,
mechanics. (The boys in Shop may actually SWEAR! What else is
new?) Take as many math and science courses as you can. If
the boys in your school have started a "Boys Only" Computer
Club, join anyway. (They don't really mean it.)

THEN, APPLY, APPLY, APPPLY

If you enjoyed your shop courses, or did well in graphics or technician programs,
apply to the top public vocational-technical schools in your area or to union apprenticeship
programs. Private vocational schools vary greatly in quality. Check out their records
before you plunk down your money. (See Appendix F for listing of some Apprenticeship
programs.)

If you did well on your school grades, or on SAT scores,
apply to leading undergraduate colleges in order to improve
your chances if you decide to go on to graduate or
professional schools. More men than women apply to the top
undergraduate institutions, so more men are admitted. (See
Appendix D for listing of leading research universities.)

SUMMARY

If you haven't seen "Stand and Deliver", run down to the nearest walk-in. The father of the brightest girl in the class wants her to quit school to work full-time in the family pizza parlor. The old man resists, but eventually comes around. If those *barrio* kids, in a run-down high school in Los Angeles can do it, so can you.

: You have a choice:

1. Buckle down while you're young and learn some skills which you can sell to the public, or to an employer,
OR
2. Lean back and take it easy in your teens--and spend the rest of your life running a stitching machine, or waiting on tables, or straining your eyes on a VDT.

18

[1] 1983 Handbook, Table III-1 , p.82; CPR, P-60, No.159, pp.100-101..

[2] Boston Globe 11/2/87.

[3] 1988 Statistical Abstract t.642, p. 389.

[4] Diana Pearce, "Toil and Trouble: Women Workers and Unemployment Compensation", Signs, Vol.10 No.3, p.456.

[5] Social Security Bulletin, January 1989, Table 5.6; pp. 18-19.

[6] U.S. Department of Health and Human Services, Vital Statistics of the United States, 1984, Volume II: Mortality, Part A (Washington, D.C.: U.SS. Government Printing Office, 1987,)\

[7] J. Laing, H. Engen, J. Maxey, American College Testing Research Report Series 87-3 "Relationship beetween ACT Scores and High School Courses", p.7, T.1.   See also : Blanche Fitzpatrick, Women's Inferior Education: An Economic Analysis, New York, Praeger Publishers, 1976, p.5   (Reprinted 1987: Pemberton Publishers, P.O. Box 441558, Somerville, MA 02144.)

[8] Gila Hanna, Ontario Institute for Studies in Education. Quoted in Boston Globe 2/13/88, p.3.

[9] Quoted in J. Ehrhart and B. Sandler, "Looking for more than a few good women in traditionally male fields". Washington, D.C. Association of American Collegees, 1818 R Strcect., N.W.   January 1987, p.4.

[10] FairTest "Is the SAT Biased?" May 1989. 342 Broadway, Cambridge, MA.02139; J. Loewen, P. Rosser, J. Katzman, "Gender Bias in SAT Items". Paper for the American Educational Research Association annual meeting, April, 1988; W. Glaberson "U.S. Court t Says Awards Based on S>A>T>'s Are Unfair to Girls", New York Times ,2/4/89.

[11] Boston Globe, 5/17/83.

[12] Boston Globe 5/18/88.

[13] Boston Globe, 8/6/87.

[14] Patrricia Cross, Beyond the Open Door (San Francisco, Jossey Bass, 1971; Table I, p.20.

[15] New York Times, 12/20/82

[16] Ellen Goodman, Boston Globe 7/9/74, p.15.

[17] U.S. General Accounting Office "What is the role of federal assistance in vocational education?" (Washington, D.C.,U.S. Government Printing Office)12/31/74, p.86.

[18] Alice deRivera in Sisterhood is Powerful, Robin Morgan (ed) .New York: Vintage Books, 1970) pp.366-75.

[19] U.S. Congress, House of Representatives, "Hearings before the Special Subcommittee on Education and Labor, 91st Congress, 2nd Session, "Discrimination Against Women" Section 805 of HR 16058, Parts 1 and 2.

[20] U.S. Department of Labor, Monthly Labor Review, August 1974, p.50.

[21] John Touhey, "Effects of Additional Women Professionals on Ratings of Occupational Prestige and Desirability". Journal of Personal ity and Social Psychology, Vol. 29, No. 1, 1974, pp.86-89.

[22] Philip Goldberg, TransActions, April 1968, pp.28-30.

[23] M. Paludi, W. B auer Sex Roles, Vol. 9, No. 3, 1983 pp.389-90.

[24] J.Grasso, J. Shea, Vocational Education and Training: impact on youth, Berleley, CA: Carnegie Council on Policy Studies in Higher Education, 1979, p.21,

[25] P. Meyer, P. Maes "The Reproduction of Occupational Segregation Among Young Women" Industrial Relations , Vol.22, No. 1 Winter 19983, pp.115-124.

[26] Institute for Equality in Education (1982). Quoted in N.O.W. Legal Defense and Education Fund release. (1982. 99 H udson Street, New York, 10013.)

[27] Philip Bennett, "Just a Paycheck, Not an Opportunity", Boston Globe12/15/85, p.15.

CHAPTER III

BRINGING UP BABIES

Unlike earlier periods of history, marriage is no longer essential as a mealticket for single women. The growth of opportunities for paid jobs means that a woman is usually able to provide at least a minimum of her own requirements for food, clothing and shelter. Yet the majority of women will marry and have children. This makes the question of economic survival much more difficult.

All you light-hearted young things, planning marriage and parenthood, (OR NOT PLANNING AT ALL)--LISTEN UP!

Once a woman has children, she does not have the option to discontinue feeding, clothing or caring for them. If you get tired of having your three dogs and five cats around, you may deep six them, but both parents are legally responsible for the neglect of children. In practice, if divorce occurs, the mother is most likely to be awarded the care of any children. In fact, many divorcing mothers are so distraught

at the possibility that their petition for custody may be
contested by the father that they sacrifice property
settlements, or support payments, to insure that he will not
compete for custody. But, in cold fact, to be awarded
custody is to be awarded a handicap in the struggle to make a
living.

You cannot leave an infant at home alone; it is
dangerous to leave children under 6 at home alone; it is
probably unwise to leave children under 12 unsupervised; and
teenagers (are you listening?) can get into a peck of trouble
very easily. Then why don't mothers stay at home with their
children? THEY NEED THE MONEY TO SURVIVE. (See Chart 3-1)

So far the federal government has refused to make a
commitment to provide public funds for day care; state
budgets are stretched to the limit, yet there are pitifully
few subsidized slots for working mothers. Even Secretary of
Labor William Brock, appearing on "Face the Nation" (on
Mother's Day) pointed out, "With more than half the nation's
mothers now in the workforce, the lack of standardized day
care has created less productive workers who spend too much
time at the office worrying about their children" [1] and he
noted that the United States is one of only two
industrialized nations (the other is South Africa) without a
nationally-funded day care program. As a result, in a study
of stress among workers, the highest stress was noted among
married women in clerical jobs; they had double the risk of
heart disease compared to other working women or housewives.[2]
It is not surprising that mothers of school-age children may
agonize over the safety of latch-key children returning to
empty apartments, often necessarily in low rent areas where
criminal activity and drug-dealing abound.

THE PROBLEM: In 1987, one of every seven women in the labor
force had a husband whose 1986 income was less
than $15,000. See Chart 3-1.[3]

In 1985, there was one divorce recorded for
every two marriages.[4]

By age 50, about one woman in 10 will be
widowed.[5]

In 1985, of the mothers awarded child support
due in 1985, only half received full payment.
About 1/4 of the mothers awarded support
received only partial payment; about 1/4
received NOTHING.[6] Thus, in most cases, it is
the divorced, separated, or never-married
mother who must provide, from her usually low-
paid job, the bulk of the children's support.

So, the problems are:
a)   How can you get a job which will support your children
       and yourself?
b)   How can you find reliable day care for the children
       while you are working?
c)   How can your family survive on Welfare payments (AFDC)
       if that becomes necessary?

              *   *   *   *   *   *   *   *

How you can cope: Finding a job which will support you and
     your children.

     The last chapter pointed out the importance of having
high-level skill training, or a good academic education
beyond high school, in order to get a better-paying job. But
supposing you neglected to do that before you had the
children--what then?

     The first step is to check with the state Employment
Service; offices are located in most of the larger cities in
each state. Find out what jobs are available and what the
pay rates are. If you are not qualified for the better-
paying jobs, find out what training slots are available, and
sign up for a program which will give you the necessary
skills. Publicly-funded day care spaces are often (but not
always) provided for women in training programs, in order to
reduce the public expenditure on welfare benefits.

     Before you take a job, find out what employer benefits
are provided by way of sick leave, as well as health and
disability insurance; and whether the employer has any
provisions for child care for workers, and if the job will be
permanent.   (The 1988 Family Security Act (welfare reform)
may help on the problem of risking the loss of welfare
benefits by taking employment which is only
short term.)   Also, it is important to try for long-term
employment so that you may be eligible for Unemployment
Compensation; state laws vary, but a basic minimum of six
months of covered employment may be required in order for you
to be eligible for Unemployment Compensation.(See Chapter V)

Chart 3-1

Most women work
because of economic need

Women in the Labor Force, March 1987

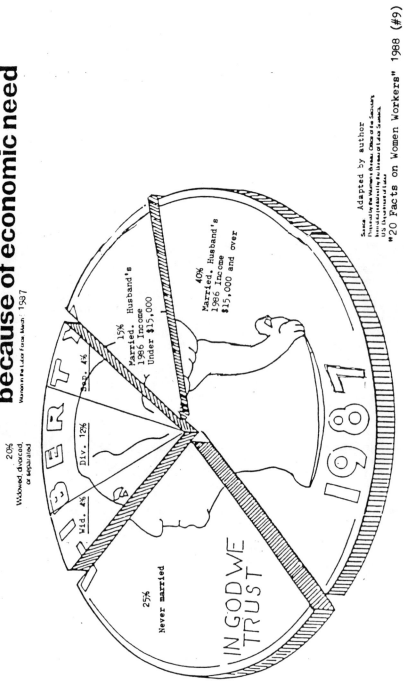

20%
Widowed, divorced,
or separated

LIBERTY

Wid. 4%   Div. 12%   Sep. 4%

15%
Married. Husband's
1986 Income
Under $15,000

40%
Married. Husband's
1986 Income
$15,000 and over

1987

25%
Never married

IN GOD WE
TRUST

Source: Adapted by author
Prepared by the Women's Bureau, Office of the Secretary
from data published by the U.S. Bureau of Labor Statistics,
U.S. Department of Labor

"20 Facts on Women Workers" 1988 (#9)

It is important to work with other women in similar
situations, or with organized women's groups, to obtain
needed changes in state funding. Insufficient child care
funding hinders women from participation in public training
programs and thereby excludes them from jobs <u>which pay enough
to support a family.</u>

b)   Child Care

Sympathy without relief
Is like mustard without beef

Where's the beef? Only about 11% of all U. S. companies
offer child care benefits.[7] Child care in the United States
is often a patchwork of day-to-day arrangements, made by
harried mothers, with relatives, friends or family day care
providers. The larger, better equipped day care centers,
with professional staffs, cost more than the average woman
worker can afford. Once upon a time, grandmothers were at
home, and sometimes able and willing to care for
grandchildren. But as financial pressures increase upon
older women, they too must find work to pay the rent. When
your best friend gets pregnant again, she won't be able to

take your toddler; or when her husband gets a job elsewhere, or when the family day care center closes because the woman who runs it needs an operation--YOU have to get cracking and find another place. You want a place that's not too expensive; where they will treat the children kindly; won't park them in front of TV all day long; won't have numerous dogs and cats competing for space; won't have child molesters on the payroll--YOU have to check out these places before or after work. Why doesn't the State inspect and control these facilities? Because child care has been such a low priority item that state budgets do not allot enough money for even minimal oversight.

If children become ill, or may infect other children with colds or flu, the day care provider may ask that they be kept at home. Then YOU must find a convalescent facility that will take them in or miss work to take care of them at home--with a likely reduction of your paycheck as well as adversely affecting job performance-ratings, promotion possibilities, and even job security. (The U.S .Congress in 1990 passed a Parental and Medical Leave bill which would have provided (unpaid) leave for employees in larger firms when they were needed at home to care for sick children or relatives; this bill was vetoed by President Bush. All voters should urge their Representatives and Senators to recognize the great need for such legislation.)

Where is your husband in all this? Probably bringing home the bacon, usually working a 40-hour week, or sometimes more. His paycheck is likely to be larger than yours, especially if you work part-time so that you yourself can care for the children part of the time. (You've heard of Catch 22?) In 1988, half the low-income families in Massachusetts paid 10% or more of their gross income for child care; 39% paid 15% or more, according to the Massachusetts Department of Human Services. [8]

Even if both of you work full time and even though younger husbands have accepted some of the responsibility for home duties, women usually do most of the cooking, cleaning and child care. Many recent studies show that working wives and husbands do not share equally in household tasks. According to one recent study, a working wife is likely to spend twice as many hours as her unemployed husband on home duties.[9]

If you are divorced, even if your ex-husband has been ordered to pay child support, and is faithful in making the full payments, on time,the cost of child care alone typically exceeds the child support award, according to sociologist Karen Seal. [10] And millions of women awarded child support payments receive partial payment or none at all.

State and federal laws are just beginning to assist the ex-wife to track down and obtain child support payments from her former husband, but especially when the man has re-married, there is often prolongèd stalling, or outright default. DO NOT GIVE UP the rights of your child to financial support from his father. This problem area is discussed in Chapter Five.

How you can cope: Finding reliable child care

Go to your city or town or county officials; if not too far to travel, visit the State Office for Children. Get any listings or ratings for day care centers in your area. DO NOT BE DISCOURAGED if officials report that neither day care slots nor public funds are available.

JOIN WITH OTHER YOUNG PARENTS in the same situation and hang in there until public officials and the public in general recognize the problem and provide some answers . Because the great spurt in the number of mothers working has happened in the past 20 years, the bureaucracy has not addressed the problem. And because mothers with small children are only a small and changing group within society, the pressure has been only intermittent; in 10 years the mother of an 8-year old no longer has the problem, and a new harried mother of an 8-year old must begin to look for answers. The problems of providing home care (for elderly relatives as well as young children) have long been recognized in other industrialized societies. Voter pressure is needed to get the attention of legislators.

JOIN A WOMEN'S GROUP which is pressuring politicians for more federal and state funds for day care.

Working mothers are supporting or helping to support the next generation (of workers, soldiers, scientists) and for this public service, publicly-funded day care is a necessity.

c)   Surviving on Welfare (AFDC) Payments

"I hated welfare but I didn't have a choice" - a Puerto Rican immigrant at age 18, who married and had three children here. Her husband was frequently unemployed. (She is now employed.)

"I hated going on Welfare. People have this conception that if you're on welfare, you're lazy and all you want is handouts. I would never tell anyone I was on Welfare because

I have a certain feeling about myself." (If day care had been available she would never have left the workforce, she said.) "It was just me and I wasn't sure how I was going to manage with just me and a newborn, but I couldn't find anyone to take care of her." a white mother of one child (now employed).

"I feel better about myself just because I'm working now." - a black mother of two sons. (now employed.)[11]

In the long run, the family is much better off, financially and otherwise, if the mother can improve her skills, obtain good child care, and get a job with adequate pay rather than to rely on Welfare payments. In 1988, there was no state in which combined AFDC and food stamps equaled 100% of the poverty level. Thirty-five states have benefit levels that are less than the needs standard set by the state itself[12]_. Admittedly, many low-income taxpayers are themselves just scraping by, and higher welfare benefits would be a burden to these tax-paying "working poor" (One solution would be for the government to spend less on $600 toilet seats, and unworkable "Star Wars" programs.and use the resulting savings to expand state funding for the support of the next generation.)

Yet in some situations where there is a small child or children to be cared for, temporary reliance on welfare payments is the only possibility; AFDC payments can provide a bridge to self-sufficiency.

It is important for you to realize that the job you obtain must pay enough not only to provide for daily needs -- food, clothing, shelter -- but ALSO provide the fringe benefits to handle health or other emergencies. AFDC benefits carry with them supplemental food stamps, possibility of subsidized rentals, and Medicaid coverage for illness of family members. You should make sure that your eligibility for these benefits is not lost while you enter a training program or other educational activity; and when you take a new job, there may be a delay before you become eligible for employer-provided health and disability insurance. The 1988 Family Security Act, sponsored by Senator Moynihan (D-NY), is intended to give women opportunities for job training and provide Day Care slots to make it possible. This is the first comprehensive welfare reform bill in 50 years, but the law has not yet been fully tested in practice.

c) How you can cope: Dealing with the Welfare System.

Once again, it is important to work with other mothers or women's groups to obtain adequate benefits for the support of your children. Without the willingness of women to bear children, and to care for them in childhood, <u>humans would disappear from the earth in less than 100 years</u>. (Let's all Save the Whales BUT...)

SUMMARY

Society recognizes the mother's achievement in poems, sentimental songs and flowers on Mother's Day, but the creation of another human being does not end with the momentous experience of birth. The child must be fed, clothed, sheltered and educated, for a good part of the next 20 years. The United States, in sorry company with South Africa, has not recognized the needs of women and children, and governmental policy has opposed adequate payment to a mother to provide for her own children (foster parents are usually much better compensated.)

If the new mother has a partner who can provide sufficient income, she is fortunate. But single parents, whether widowed, divorced, separated, or never-married, or women whose husband's work is irregular or low-paid, are left to improvise solutions on their own. In the United States in 1986, there were 4 million families on AFDC, including 7 million children [13] -- women and their children are the overwhelming majority of those often held up to scorn as "welfare drones."

"We are the world- we are the children" is more than a catchy tune. The American public has not understood the problems facing the single parent, working for pay or at home. All women need to work and vote together in order to pressure legislators and public officials to provide women with the help they need in order to properly care for our children.

[1] William Brock, U.S. Secretary of Labor, quoted in the <u>Boston Globe 5/12/86</u>

[2] National Heart, Lung and Blood Institute: Study of Framingham,. MA; quoted in Boston Globe 1/25/80

[3] U.S. Department of Labor, Women's Bureau, "Facts About Women," 88-2, #9.

[4] <u>1988 Statistical Abstract,</u> Table 59

[5] <u>1988 Statistical Abstract,</u> Table 48

[6] U.S. Department of Commerce, Bureau of the Census, "Child Support and Alimony, 1985", Series P-23, No. 152, Washington, D.C., U.S. Government Printing Office, pp.1-2

[7] <u>Boston Globe 2/26/88</u>

[8] Massachusetts Department of Human Services, "The Economics of Child Care in Massachusetts", Boston, MA. State House, 1988, p.vii.

[9] V. Nieva,"Work and Family Linkages" in <u>Women and Work,</u> L. Larwood etal (eds) Berkeley, CA. Sage Publications, 1985.

[10] K.Seal, "A Decade of No-Fault Divorce", <u>*Family Advocate*</u>, Volume 1, No. 4, Spring 1979pp.10-14. (Cited in Weitzman, p.271)

[11] Boston Globe, 10/8/84; pp.1,20-22.

[12] Center on Social Welfare Policy and Law, "Analysis of 1988 Benefit Levels in the Program of Aid to Families with Dependent Children". Washington, D>C> 1029 Vermont Avenue, N.W. (1988) p.1

[13] <u>1988 Statistical Abstract</u>, Table 588, p.353.

Chapter IV

GETTING <u>LESS</u> FOR YOUR MONEY

MOM, SINCE YOU ONLY MAKE 62¢ ON THE DOLLAR, IT'S GONNA COST YOU TWICE AS MUCH TO BUY PARK PLACE.

SHERRIE
SHEPHERD

Reprinted by Permission of UFS Inc.

Out of the mouths of babes..! Are these little cherubs onto something?

If a person earns $1000 a month, it costs him/her about two weeks of work to pay for a $500 a month apartment rental.

If a person earns $2000 a month, it costs him/her only one week's work to pay for that same apartment.

Using the earnings distribution reported in Chapter Two, it is not hard to guess whether it is he or she who is more likely to be earning the smaller amount. That's one way of looking at consumer problems. But we usually think in terms of prices. Is it possible that women will be charged higher prices than a man for the same item, or otherwise disadvantaged as a consumer?

. All of us, men and women alike, are the targets (victims?) of high-pressure advertising campaigns. If women are pursued more intensely by cosmetic manufacturers, men are bombarded by ads for super automobiles and trucks. Yet, even though some of the evidence is anecdotal, rather than from broad-based scientific studies, each of us may be able to report instances of price discrimination based on the sex of the customer.

For example, one of my students tried an experiment involving prices for cleansing. Enlisting the help of her boyfriend, she and he checked out local cleansing shops, using the same shirt and slacks in each outlet. For the same items, she was frequently quoted a higher price. Another student, who worked part-time in a department store, found a high priced line of sweaters sold for both the men and women, identical except for larger sizes in the men's department. The sweaters cost several dollars more in women's sizes. Women's jeans, usually smaller, were also reported at higher prices than men's jeans from the same manufacturer. A complaint was filed in 1987 with the Massachusetts Commission Against Discrimination charging that many department stores in the Springfield area, including Sears and Penney's, charged women more than men for alterations; one store owner wrote to the complainants explaining that higher charges on alterations for female clothing were "standard industry practice."[1]

We must recognize that in some situations it may cost a manufacturer or cleanser MORE to work on SMALLER sizes -- but in general it is likely less thread, fabric, and labor would be required for smaller items. The few dollars at stake in each case may seem like pretty small potatoes. But when we consider that the average woman earns much less than the average man, such price differences worsen the economic situation of women relative to men. Women consumers are at a disadvantage:

a. in what they are able to afford (access to credit for purchase of a home, car or other major item), and in their acceptability as tenants.
b. in making decisions as to the necessity or safety of medical treatment or drugs prescribed.
c. in the availability of insurance, as well as the rates they are charged, to protect themselves and their families against expenses of illness and to replace income lost due to disability or old age.

In the following sections, we will look at each of these problems in turn and suggest ways you can cope with them.

a. Credit access and housing

THE PROBLEM: Women have greater difficulty in obtaining credit for car loans or housing mortgages, than a man with the same income; "women find that landlords will take a pet before he's going to take a child.' [2]

We are not talking about the bad old days, when a
married woman was not viewed by the law as an individual
person, and when her property and income would be controlled
by her husband. There are now laws requiring non-
discriminatory credit access in many states, in addition to
the federal Equal Credit Opportunity law (passed in 1976)
which forbids asking a woman credit applicant about plans for
children and mandates that alimony and child support must be
accepted as well as other sources of income. Yet, in the
1980's divorced women continued to be denied car loans or
credit cards in their own name even when they have had a long
working history, sometimes as the only breadwinner with a
student husband. In 1986, investigators for the Federal
Trade Commission reported "a great reluctance" on the part of
lenders to base credit on other than employment income.i.e.,
on alimony or child support. It may be impossible to prove
that illegal sex discrimination is involved in many cases,
because a lender can lawfully reject an application for "a
bare credit history" -- that is, if the credit during
marriage was recorded in the husband's name only. One
student reported that her grandmother returned from her
husband's funeral only to find a letter from the credit card
company demanding the immediate return of the husband's card!

In 1983, a young woman started a service business in
Minnesota. In 1984 she had gross revenues of over $1
million, employing 13 people. When she sought a business
loan, one bank denied the request, citing insufficient
collateral. Another bank offered a loan at a high rate,
required collateral twice the loan amount, and her father's
guarantee.[3] Other business women surveyed by the Woman's
Equity Action League reported being offered discriminatory
terms; almost one third were asked for their spouse's
signature. The woman with the million dollar business
reported that the bank official "agreed that I had to go
through much more than a man to get a loan and said 'That's
just the way things are!'"[4]

Common sense tells us that lenders who want to stay in
the lending business are interested in the prospect that the
loan will be repaid. We have seen that women predominate in
low-paying industries and occupations, in insurance, clothing
manufacture, food service, working as clerks, stitchers,
waitresses -- while men are the majority of employees in
higher-paid trucking, automobile manufacturing, construction,
and in the higher-income professions. Thus it is
understandable that women are more likely than men to have a
problem of obtaining credit.

Yet without a car loan, women may be unable to accept
employment in suburban areas; even more burdensome, women may

be denied mortgage funding to permit the purchase of a decent home for their families.

Women also experience greater difficulty in renting an apartment. How often can the newly-widowed or divorced woman come up with "first month, plus last month, or security deposit"? And if a woman listens to her heart rather than her head, and seeks custody of the children, even makes concessions to her divorced husband in order to achieve custody of small children -- her chances of finding an affordable rental in a safe neighborhood are diminished by their presence. At the 1975 hearings of the U. S. Department of Housing and Urban Development, one realtor testified that "The least wanted tenants are women -- elderly women and single women with children."[5]

Minorities and single women are not shown all the available housing, according to complaints filed with the Massachusetts Commission Against Discrimination, which charged real estate agents in three Massachusetts cities in 1985. "'Women on welfare were...told they would have to pay higher rents or make larger security deposits' according to Investigating Commissioner Allen of the MCAD. 'That would take them out of the housing market.'"[6] . .The woman alone with the child or children really has the worst time of all because of the entanglement of all kinds of discrimination, the layers of discrimination... if the woman is of a minority group, it adds another layer,.... and if she's got a large family, it adds another; it becomes impossible."[7] Of course children can be destructive, or noisy, or just generally pesty - we were all young once.

Thus, as compared to the average young man, the average young woman is more limited in her choice of major consumer goods, because of the difficulty she may encounter in obtaining credit. The testimony of women in the Federal Housing and Urban Development hearings, as well as individual accounts of women bringing complaints to state Equal Opportunity Commissions confirm the continuing problem of credit access for women, and of unequal access to desirable housing.

What you can do to cope with credit barriers:

As the old adage goes, the best way to qualify for a loan is not to need one; such a happy state suggests that you would have reached a certain age, hold a well-paid job, and own some valuable assets including a solid savings account. But--you need it NOW! What can be done? If you believe you have been denied credit because of your sex (or age, race, ethnic origin) -- tell the bank, auto dealer, mortgage lender or consumer credit agency that you will seek redress through state and federal agencies, if you are denied equal access to

credit or housing. Then, of course, after you have obtained
the credit or housing, keep your payments current and build a
good credit rating. If you have a temporary interruption in
income, because of unemployment, illness, or family crisis,
get in touch with the lender or landlord, and make
arrangements to adjust the payment schedule. So ---know your
rights and use them. (See Appendix B)

NOTE: It is important that a woman apply for credit in her
own name: as Jane Smith, not Mrs. John Smith.

b. Medical Care:

THE PROBLEM: Women are more likely than men to be exposed to
            unnecessary operations; to be prescribed
            addictive drugs; to be exposed to unsafe
            products not adequately tested by government
            agencies.

b.1 "Unnecessary surgery

     The germs are out to get you whether you are a boy or
girl, woman or man. But when it comes to medical care
females are the major consumers. In 1985, government
statistics show 16,000 operations for females, compared to
9,000 for males.[8] As mentioned in Chapter Two, women actually
surpass men in activities requiring endurance -- marathons,
long-distance swims -- and there are several millions more
older women than older men. Then why should women be more
likely than men to undergo operations?

     As shown in Chapter Two, women are a small minority of
practicing doctors, and an even smaller percentage of
surgeons. Women have been brought up in a society where the
major authority figures -- high school and college
administrators, bosses in business, and political leaders --
are usually male. Should it be surprising that the doctor's
judgment on the necessity of an operation is less likely to
be questioned by a female than by a male patient?   A number
of studies have indicated that many "women's" operations are
unnecessary. Young surgeons, often with burdensome education
loans to repay, and with few patients when they begin
practice, may be inclined to err on the side of performing an
operation, even when the evidence of need is not
overwhelming. As one general practitioner noted: "Hospital
coffee shops are full of young surgeons waiting around for a
case," [9] (And,in fairness, fear of malpractice suits may also
provide an incentive.)

     Yet a study by Columbia University School of Public
Health found that one-third of hysterectomies had been
unnecessary, and seriously questioned the necessity of half
the Caesareans performed; (in 1984 one-fifth of all
deliveries were by Caesarean section, more than four times
the 1965 rate.)

     "An appalling number of patients aged 20 to 29
undergoing hysterectomies had no disease whatsoever".. Only
about one-third of operations leading to female sterilization
were found to be medically warranted.[10]

If automobile dealers had the power to suggest that purchase of a new car was necessary to save your life, there would presumably be many more automobiles sold; physicians and surgeons have a unique ability to create demand for their services. Third party payment - Blue Cross/Blue Shield, Medicare and Medicaid - guarantees payment for the patient who works for a company which provides group health insurance, for the elderly, or the poor WHETHER OR NOT there is a medical necessity for operations, treatments, or frequent checkups. Because doctors, like the rest of mortals, are interested in their income level; AND because women, after a lifetime in a system which provides male authority figures in the home, at school and at work, may be more easily persuaded than men are to "consume" more medical care - it is understandable that women are likely to make more frequent visits to physicians, to undergo more operations, and to be prescribed more drugs. Money spent on medical care cannot be spent on other items, further restricting women's spending choices.

And the darker side of the coin, paradoxically, is that millions of women in low-paid or part-time jobs, or divorced or widowed women, who are not covered by employer-provided group insurance, and who cannot afford the high individual rates charged women for individual health insurance, may be going without needed medical care or surgery. "Women in their forties and fifties must often empty their pockets to pay for routine preventive procedures. Midlife women without private health insurance...purchase significantly less health care than women with insurance. There is no evidence that the medical needs of uninsured midlife women are any less.than those of insured women of the same age." [11]

b. 2 Prescription Drugs

Not only do women undergo more operations than do men (some, apparently, unnecessary) women are more often prescribed drugs. In a number of studies women are shown to be twice as likely as men to use prescription drugs.[12] Why should this be so? Well, as mentioned above, women make more visits to the doctor. Their complaints may often be vague: perhaps a suburban wife and mother cut off from adult companionship; or a "superwoman" combining a paid job with the management of a family; or a single mother coping with the problems of working and finding reliable child care. Of course, hardworking husbands and fathers "bringing home the bacon" also have to deal with stress. While for men an after work drink may help to calm tension, women up to now have been less inclined to "belly up to the bar" (though some may have become their own bartenders in the privacy of the laundry room.) For many women, a doctor's prescription represents a validation of a claim to a physical problem, as well as providing, a chemical escape from the burdens of her everyday life. Yet prescription drug consumption creates the problems of gradual addiction, for "ordinary housewives" and "working mothers" as well as for the celebrities, for Betty Ford or Elizabeth Taylor.

Why would a competent and honorable physician prescribe such potentially dangerous medication? Well, consider the situation of the general practitioner or internist looking out at a packed waiting room, mostly women, waiting to report a problem beyond the power of the doctor to solve. The problem results from the conditions of her life. The doctor cannot provide a solution to the family money problems, or lack of reliable child care, or the pressures of combining paid jobs and home upkeep. A major drug company in advertisements addressed to the physician, in professional magazines, suggested with reference to the trapped housewife:

"You can't set her free, but you can help her feel less anxious." Put more bluntly: "Shoot her up to shut her up"; by prescribing a drug, the physician can not only shorten the average time spent with each patient, he can also often earn the gratitude of that patient.[13] One doctor responded to a researcher:

"When a woman comes to me, she doesn't feel well. When she leaves me she expects to leave with something that will assure that she'll feel better. If I don't provide it for her, you can bet she'll find someone who will.[14]

Again, as with other expenditures on medical care (not covered by health insurance, especially for women in low-paid employment) women are restricted in their living standards to the extent that a larger portion of income must be spent on doctor's bills or drugs.

b.3 Dangerous products

In some areas it is not possible to be a shrewd comparison shopper. When products must be tested for safety, or for toxic substances, the average consumer, man or woman, must rely on government agencies for protection. There seems to have been low priority given to checking products used exclusively by women, when compared to the action taken to recall a dangerous food product, or a defective automobile.

For example, from 1971 to 1974 A. H. Robins Company sold millions of intrauterine contraceptive devices (IUD) before the Food and Drug Administration ordered sales suspended. The company filed for bankruptcy in August 1985 after 14,000 shield-related lawsuits had been initiated. Thousands of women who became pregnant despite the shield, miscarried; others gave birth to deformed children, and others became unable to bear children. More than 30 women in the United States are known to have died of resulting infections. In 1986 G. D. Searle, the last major American manufacturer of intrauterine devices withdrew them from the American market, after almost 800 lawsuits had been filed, charging the devices had caused perforation of the uterus, pelvic inflammatory disease, sterility, or dangerous ectopic pregnancies.[15]

Amendments made in 1976 to the Food, Drug and Cosmetic Act excused from pre-market testing tampons made with new and potentially dangerous synthetic substances, on the grounds that they were equivalent to devices already being sold. As a result, many young women died as a result of Toxic Shock Syndrome.

How you can cope with the problem of medical and drug expense and product safety:

First, don't accept one doctor's opinion as final. Even though most doctors are decent, competent and conscientious, a second opinion on an operation is worth getting. (A second opinion is often covered, or even required, by group health insurance policies.)

The second, but equally important point, is that you should make every effort to find a job which PROVIDES health insurance, as well as good pay.

AND, IF you have more to do every day than is humanly possible -- and that describes most mothers of young children with a job, child care, or other family problems -- DON'T

ACCEPT DRUGS as the solution. Change your job! Find a counsellor at church or family agencies in your area! JOIN with other young parents to create public pressure for more child care facilities. That is, work to correct the problem, rather than try to forget it via pill popping; just meeting other women who share your problem is a help!

Also, JOIN WITH OTHER WOMEN to pressure public agencies, such as the Food and Drug Agency or the Environmental Protection Agency to be vigilant in checking products for toxic substances, or in testing air, water, and soil for pollutants which may harm your health or the health of family members.

c. Insurance

PROBLEM; Over a lifetime a woman who has automobile, health,
disability and life insurance, and an annuity, purchased as
an individual, will pay substantially more than a man for
identical coverage.

     The insurance industry continues to fight tooth and
nail against "unisex" insurance, under which men and women
would be charged the same rates. On some types of insurance,
life insurance, and auto insurance for young women, women may
pay lower "rates"; on other types of insurance, individual
health and disability insurance, and retirement annuities
women pay more than men do. The insurance companies argue
that to charge men and women the same rate for the various
coverages would be costly to women, because they would lose
on some of the lower rates mentioned above. We are probably
safe in assuming, however, that the insurance companies, like
any other business, are fighting not to protect women from
higher prices, but rather to protect their own substantial
profits from the present system. And in fact, if we look at
the situation more closely, some of the "lower" rates for
women are an illusion; because women generally purchase small
dollar amounts of life insurance, the return per insurance
dollar spent is lower.

     Only one state so far, Montana, has passed a law
requiring "unisex" rates -- the sky has not fallen in the Big
Sky state. The Massachusetts Insurance Commissioner has
ordered all companies doing business in the state to cease to
make distinctions in premiums or benefits based on an
applicant's gender; Hawaii, North Carolina and Michigan have
also outlawed sex-based automobile insurance rates. But
large insurance companies continue to resist.

     To translate the above into a more understandable
picture, consider the typical woman supporting a child or
children. Nearly ten million women maintain families alone.
Because women are more likely than men to work in small firms
where the employer does not provide fringe benefits, she must
purchase individual coverage. She must consider the
likelihood that she may be unable to work because of illness
or accident. On a typical woman's salary, the high cost of
individual coverage is very likely to be more than she can
afford. If she is too ill to care for her family, she will
not be able to pay for a substitute homemaker. She cannot
afford the high individual rate to provide Blue Cross/Blue
Shield or HMO coverage for medical and surgical expenses.
For such a woman, illness or disability is more than a

financial disaster -- it is a prescription for family breakup
with unbearable worry for the mother added to the trauma of
physical disability. Most working women who are single
parents are just one paycheck away from the welfare rolls.

How you can cope with the problem of excessive insurance
rates:

     Join with other women to pressure your state legislature
to mandate unisex rates. Even though there are more very-
long-lived women than there are men, for most women mortality
rates are similar to those for men. Yet under the present
sex-differentiated system, the burden of providing private
pensions to the exceptionally long-lived woman is borne only
by other women.[16] Under a unisex system, all of us, men and
women, would share equally the cost of supporting long-lived
individuals of both sexes.

     Join with other voters to urge passage of a federal law
guaranteeing Universal Health coverage for all. In 1988,
Massachusetts enacted a law providing Universal Health Care,
but state-by -state passage would be a long process.
(Remember the Equal Rights Amendment -- many state
legislatures refused to ratify it). The United States has
lagged behind other industrialized countries in this and
related areas (infant mortality, child care, paid maternity
leave); we usually find ourselves in the dubious company of
South Africa. For the typical low-paid woman, publicly-
subsidized health insurance is an absolute necessity.
Until the present insurance system is reformed, your best bet
is to shop around for insurance. Many states have Consumer
Affairs Departments which can provide advice or pamphlets to
help you get your money's worth in insurance coverage.

     When job-hunting, check to see whether a prospective
employer provides health, disability or other insurance, and
look into the set-up of the pension program to make sure that
men and women receive equal benefits on retirement. If you
have been divorced, be sure to check with your former
husband's company to determine the amount you will need to
pay to continue coverage for you and your family under his
group plan. Under federal law, women and their families now
have the right to continue in the company insurance programs
for three years after divorce or widowhood. (After that
period is over, however, the very high rates charged to women
for individual health and disability plans again become a
serious barrier to protection for women heading families.)
Although you personally may not have this problem at the
moment, any young woman should realize that she may be
supporting children some day, and should work with organized
women's groups to provide support to those now struggling
with the problem.

SUMMARY

It is essential for the economic survival of women and their families that working women seek and find well-paid, steady employment. But the family standard of living also depends on whether women are charged higher prices, or must spend their limited income on unnecessary goods and services, or are denied access to insurance, credit or decent housing.

When it comes to actual price discrimination based on sex, by manufacturers or clothing stores, the old Romans had it about right : Let the buyer beware! In addition to comparison shopping (which you probably do anyway) let the manufacturer or retailer know that you object to discriminatory pricing and refuse to make purchases there until the practice is stopped.

In the 1980's women continued to be denied credit for starting up a business, or for major consumer purchases; they may be denied mortgage credit for family housing, or be rejected as tenants; they may be targeted by some in the medical field for unnecessary operations, or for excessive drug prescription, or for unsafe birth control devices; they may be charged excessive prices for health and disability insurance, and receive less than their money's worth of benefits from life or automobile insurance.

To cope with these problems, USE the anti-discrimination laws now in force at local, state or federal levels, to obtain your rights from credit companies, banks, or real estate agencies (Appendix B); get a second opinion whenever surgery is suggested, and take action to cut back your overcrowded schedule rather than trying to relieve daily pressure through prescription drugs; through the local social agencies, or the state Children's Bureau, look for better child care options; check your state Consumer Affairs Department for any adverse information on drugs or birth control devices; ask the state Insurance Commissioner's office for information on comparative rates of insurance companies; work with other parents to get publicly-subsidized, state-inspected, quality child care. Women's organizations in your city or state can often provide useful information.

AND - JOIN OTHER WOMEN in working to pressure legislators and city officials to recognize the problems of women and their children in areas relating to health and safety; let your U. S. Representatives and Senators know that basic health care for every American citizen should be guaranteed by U. S. law.

44

[1] Massachusetts N.O.W. News, Spring 1987. Boston, MA: Massachusetts N.O.W., p.5.

[2] National Council of Negro Women, Inc. Women and Housing: A report on sex discrimination in 5 American cities. (Atlanta, St. Louis, San Antonio, San Francisco, Washington, D.C.) U>S> Department of Housing and Urban Development. Washington, D.C. :U.S. Government Printing Office, 1975. p.37.

[3] Gillian Rudd, National Association of Women Business Owners, quoted in Women's Equity Action League WEAL Washington Report, June-July 1986, p.7.

[4] WEAL Washington Report, June-July 1986, p.8.

[5] Women and Housing. op cit., p.34.

[6] Boston Globe, 4/29/86

[7] Women and Housing, op.cit. p.83

[8] 1988 Statistical Abstract, p.100, T.157.

[9] Edwin Blackstone, "Misallocation of Medical Resources", Public Policy 22 (3) Summer 19974, pp.329-352.

[10] New York Times 8/11/86.

[11] Older Women's League OWL Observer May-June 1987.

[12] Verbrugge and Steiner. "Prescribing Drugs to Men and Women", Health Psychology 1985 4 (1) pp.79-98.

[13] Czekaj, Corinna "Women and Drugs". (Unpublished paper by student, Goucher College, 1981. (Quoting from Charlotte Muller "The Overmedicated Society", Science June 5, 1972.

[14] M. Nellis. The Female Fix . Boston, MA. Houghton MIfflin, 1980 , p.92.

[15] M. Mintz. At Any Cost. New York: Pantheon Books, 1985; Tamar Lewin, New York Times Book Review, 1/12/86.

[16] Barbara Bergmann . "Forbidding the Use of Gender in Insurance", American Economic Association, Committee on the Status of Women in the Economics Profession, Fall , 1983.

Chapter V

WOMEN AND "the system"

So far we have been looking at ways women can take action
to give themselves and their families a better chance in
life. The suggested actions include: applying to the top
public vocational, or trade union apprentice programs, (if
your strengths and interests are in craft work or technical
skills) or to top academic colleges and universities, (if
your strengths are in academic areas); exerting pressure on
political officials, through parents' groups, to obtain
needed child care facilities; comparison shopping to get the
best value when spending a dollar; avoiding unnecessary
spending by resisting pressure by suppliers of medical and
surgical care, prescription drugs, dangerous birth control
devices or high cost insurance; using existing laws against
discriminatory credit or housing practices.

But in some areas it seems that "the cards are stacked"
against women, with a bias built into "the system". What is
"the system?" It could be defined as the legal and
institutional framework which modern society has built up
over time. Of course the great virtue of a democracy is that
each of us can work to change "the system", but change is a
slow process. For example, women did finally get the vote,
but it took almost a century of struggle. So while you're
working and waiting for the system to change, it is important
for women to recognize the built-in obstacles in their path.
That is,   D
                                                          A
                                                        E
                                                      H
                                      PLAN   A

Where does "the system" adversely affect women? A few of
the key areas of built-in disadvantage for women are listed
below. We will look at these areas in the following
sections, and suggest ways you can cope with each.

1.   Marriage and divorce arrangements; property settlements;
     alimony and child support.
2.   Unemployment
3.   Military and civil service employment
4.   Criminal justice system: women offenders; protection
     against violence
5.   Social Security System: women and old age.

In many of these areas, state and federal "systems" co-
exist; if there is a conflict, federal law holds.
Traditionally legislation dealing with family life is left to
the states, but some federal laws have been recently been
enacted (for example, with respect to fathers who default on
child support payments.) Because there are many differences
in the laws of the 50 states, as well as year-to-year changes
in the laws of some states, it is not always possible to cite
"THE law." (To find out what the law says in your own state,
check with the Women's Commission at the State House, or with
organized groups such as the National Organization for Women
in your area.) But it is possible to draw some general
conclusions about the situation of women in the areas listed
above and these may help you to avoid some of the problems,
or to handle them better.

1.   <u>Marriage and Divorce Arrangements:</u>

         (THE PROBLEM: - When divorce occurs, the wife and any
                        children generally drop to a much lower
                        standard of living, including housing..

                        Alimony is rarely awarded, even in
                        marriages of long standing.

                        Wives generally receive less than half
                        marital property.

                        Child support awarded by the courts is
                        generally inadequate, and husbands
                        frequently default, partially or
                        completely.

Weddings are a universal and generally joyous
celebration,with loving support from family and friends.
Starry-eyed young couples believe their union will last
forever, but the numbers indicate otherwise. The rising

trend of recent years leads demographers to predict that 1 in 2 current marriages will eventually end in divorce. For both husband and wife, the pressures of dual working schedules and the economic and personal costs of raising a family have made modern marriages hard to sustain. Wives and mothers today are less willing than the older generation to put up with abusive or miserly partners.

However, much we may regret the break-up of families, today it is a fact of life. For this reason, women should be aware of the way "the system" may affect their lives if divorce does occur. Because state laws differ, it is essential for you to look into laws of your own state relative to your economic rights after divorce, and if divorce is decided on, to seek advice from a lawyer specializing in this field.

Because most women marry, and the majority will have children, I would recommend that every high school woman look at a more detailed account of problems of marriage and divorce than this author can provide. Good sources are: Weitzman, The Divorce Revolution; Eisler, Dissolution; and Crites and Hepperle, Women, the Courts, and Equality. "No fault" divorce was hailed as a desirable reform when it was introduced in California in 1970, as a preferable alternative to the hypocritical staging of adulterous situations, or the filing of charges of cruelty by the partner. Amost all states now have some form of "no fault" divorce, sometimes in addition to the traditional fault-based suits, or by mutual consent, or by living apart for a specified period. As the "reform" has worked out, however, the current divorce system has been an economic disaster for the women and children involved. As shown in nationwide studies cited in the books listed above, after the divorce the husband retains the lion's share of his income, and the greater part of any marital assets

Real Property Distribution

Most middle and lower-income families have property assets limited to the family home and car, with perhaps a modest amount of savings in bank accounts and insurance. (It has been frequently pointed out - no middle-class family can really afford divorce.) The family's chief earning asset is the working husband; even if the wife has worked, she has usually been a smaller contributor to the family's cash earnings, because of the "women's jobs" she has held, and because, if there are children, her work experience may have been intermittent.

In California, and 8 other "community property" states, (Arizona, Hawaii, Idaho, Louisiana, Nevada, New Mexico, Texas and Washington) each spouse is entitled to ownership of one-half of all income and property acquired during marriage (although the husband may have the legal right to sell joint property - except real estate - without the wife's knowledge or consent.) In the other 41 "separate property" states, the

common law tradition holds that the property belongs to the
one whose name it is in, or who paid for it. Many of these
states have passed "equal" or "equitable distribution" laws,
under which the court at divorce is directed to base property
division on such factors as: length of marriage; earning
ability of each spouse, and child custody arrangements.

BUT whether "equal" or "equitable" distribution of marital
assets governs the judge's decisions in any state, the
outcome is that the economic situation of former wives (and
any children in their care) declines sharply. The California
study by Weitzman, as well as studies in New Jersey and New
York show that women tend to receive less than half the
marital property, even when there are children in their
custody.[1]

In addition to facing the physical problems associated with
moving a household, particularly with young children
included, the newly-divorced woman must cope with the
difficulty of renting (much less purchasing) a home on a par
with the one she must leave. As noted in Chapter Four, women
with children have difficulty in obtaining rental housing. A
New York attorney testifying at the HUD hearings pointed out:
"Denying housing to people with children is really
discrimination against women, since we all know the parent
with custody of the child is usually the mother. So making
this blanket rule that we don't want children or unmarried
parents is really direct discrimination against women."[2]

Intangible Property Distribution

The judges, usually, male, empowered to divide the family
assets have tended to view the husband's earning power as his
exclusive property. Yet in marriage, when children come
along, and must be cared for, it is typically the wife who
withdraws from full-time career-oriented employment. Thus,
if divorce occurs, the wife has less job experience -- track
record -- when she tries to find a job to support herself and
children. She also has on her own account, no group health
insurance, disability or life insurance; low or non-existent
contributions to public Unemployment Compensation; and
usually very little history of contributions to her own
Social Security account, or to private pension programs.

Pensions: Contributions to a company pension fund, by
employer and/or employee, are a necessary supplement to
Social Security benefits in the retirement years. Such
pension funds, built up during the years of a marriage, are a
major "joint asset", but divorced wives are not guaranteed a
share. Practically all "community property" states, and a
majority of "separate property" states, permit but DO NOT
REQUIRE courts to divide future private pension income when
divorce occurs. Former wives of Civil Service or military
personnel are not assured of a share of their ex-husband's
pension because of variations in state laws and the likely
change in residence for the military. Congressional

legislation was needed to obtain for divorced Foreign Service wives a pro-rata share of the ex-husband's pension, related to the years of marriage.

Talk of pension rights is likely to inspire a large yawn among teenagers who do not expect ever to grow old. But when you get there - you still need food, clothing and shelter. Two thirds of the poor elderly are women.[3]

Health Insurance: Even jaded federal and state legislators have been shocked by the situations reported as a result of the loss of health insurance coverage after divorce, for both ex-wives and children. This led to the passage of a federal law (COBRA, 1986) as well as laws in many states, requiring that benefits from the husband's group insurance policy be extended to the ex-wife and dependent children for some period following the divorce. Under the federal law, although divorced and widowed spouses have the right, with their children, to continue participation in the husband's policy, the women must pay both employer and employee's share of the group premium, and the coverage is limited in time. Three years down the road, and that much older, the woman must find an insurance company which will accept her, and will charge a premium she can afford. (See Chapter Four)

No healthy young woman expects to become ill, but insurance was created to provide some economic security when the unexpected happens. Until National Health Insurance becomes a reality, the loss of the husband's group insurance coverage means that many divorced women are at great risk for unprotected illness.

The likelihood of re-marriage by the former husband and the possible appearance of a second set of children, adds another complication to the problems of sharing of "career assets"* The wisdom of Solomon may be needed to make a final judgment on competing claims, but continuing to ignore the problems caused by our patchwork of laws is not likely to produce a solution. National Health Insurance would provide all citizens, young and old, with access to basic health care; in this area also, the United States has lagged behind other industrialized countries.

*("Career assets" is Weitzman's term for those assets acquired as part of a spouse's career or career potential - that is, pension and retirement benefits, medical and hospital insurance, license to practice a profession, and similar assets.)

Alimony

"A woman is not a breeding cow to be nurtured during her years of fecundity, then conveniently and economically converted to cheap steaks when past her prime."[4]

A few years back, in a course on <u>Women in the Economy</u> which I was teaching at Goucher College in Maryland, the class consisted of about 20 teen-aged women undergraduates, and three older women "returnees". Two of the older women were divorced mothers of teenagers, and the third, a little younger, had a husband and a small daughter. When alimony came up for discussion, a young single student declared, to murmured approval from her classmates, "I would NEVER take alimony." Spontaneously, the three older women broke in with "Don't be FOOLISH!" Experience does teach one never to say NEVER.

THE PROBLEM: Nationally only about 15% of all divorcing women were awarded alimony in 1986.[5]

The California study indicated that, within six months, about one in six men owed an average of $1000 of unpaid spousal support.[6]

Nationally, the average (mean) income from a alimony was about $311 per month in 1985, for those actually receiving alimony.[7] .

Generous alimony awards are part of an American myth, and a reliable source of humor. Yet, notwithstanding the experience of Johnny Carson and other celebrities, in fact alimony is often not sought (and rarely awarded if the husband has low annual earnings). Understandably, the husband's income which was barely adequate to provide food, clothing and shelter to a wife and family while the group shared one roof, cannot easily be stretched to cover two households, especially when a second family is created.

The divorced wife who chooses to work in order that she and the children can improve a poverty-level existence must usually pay for the child care herself. If she chooses to remain at home to care for the children, AND IS awarded alimony, the mean alimony payment (nationally, in 1985, $3,733 annnually,[8] equal to about $72 per week) does not compensate for the lost income from paid employment. (Even minimum wage employment in 1990 pays $152 per 40-hour week, or close to $8,000 a year.) Therefore, pride or no, the young divorced woman who accepts child support, but does not wish to file for alimony, should consider the opportunity cost of staying at home to care for children; alimony can be at least a partial replacement for job income foregone.

In summary, although younger women, especially those without children, in marriages of shorter duration, may not seek alimony, mothers of any age, caring for children, as well as older "displaced homemakers" may need alimony. We have seen (Chapter Two) that women are overwhelmingly concentrated in low-paid sectors of the labor market. The chances are slim that an older woman with little paid employment over 15 or 20 years will be able to find a good-paying job. If there are very young children to be cared for,

the problem is compounded. Not just in California, but
nationwide, the new rules for alimony have been adopted after
many women have used their productive years to care for
husband and children. Thus the substitution of a few years
of "rehabilitative alimony" deprives these women of the share
of the family economic status to which they have contributed.
As appeals Court Judge Gardner declared:

> "In those cases in which it is the decision of the parties
> that the woman becomes the homemaker, the marriage is of
> `substantial duration, and at separation the wife is to all
> intents and purposes unemployable, the husband simply has
> to face up to the fact that his support responsibilities
> are going to be of extended duration - perhaps for
> life...   This has nothing to do with feminism, sexism,
> male chauvinism, or any other trendy social ideology. It
> is ordinary common sense, basic decency and simple
> justice..."[9]

Child Support

Reprinted by Permission of UFS Inc.

> "I remembered all the years when my kids went without;
> all the quahogging and clamming for something to eat;
> standing in the pouring rain cooking on the outdoor grill
> because the electricity was shut off; dragging the vacuum
> cleaner and the kids from house to house so I could make some
> money cleaning and have them with me and safe.

> And then I stood up tall and said: "Lock him up."

(Statement by Cape Cod woman who chose jail for her ex-
husband (a plumber) who had defaulted on court-ordered child
support payments for five years.)[10]

THE PROBLEM: Women receive child custody in 9 out of 10
            uncontested divorces;[11] child support is awarded
            only 61% of the time.[12]

In 1985, of almost 9 million women in the United
States with children under 21, whose fathers
were not living at home, only 5.4 million were
awarded child support.

Of the 4.4 entitled to support in 1985, only 2
million of the mothers received full child
support payments from the absent father; one
quarter received partial payment; one quarter,
nothing at all.[13]

The first question which comes to mind is: Are the child
support awards sufficient for the needs of children in the
care of a single parent? The U.S. Department of Agriculture
in 1986 estimated that the cost of raising a child to 18,
excluding college costs is $100,000[14] a second child might be
expected to add another 50% to that figure. That figures out
to about $8,000 per year for two children; (to simplify the
figures, we assume that there is zero inflation over the 18
years.) Costs would be expected to vary between high cost
and low cost regions, or between urban and rural situations.
(At this point you might look up the Mom and Pop in your life
and say: "Hey, guys, thanks a bunch!")

For a custodial mother with two children, mean child
support in 1985 amounted to $2597 per year (including all
women who received some payment)[15] . Even in areas where
living costs are lower, the Department of Agriculture
estimates indicate a substantial shortfall between the
average child support provided, and the amount needed. For
those women receiving less than the median, or nothing at all
- Disaster!

The situation for custodial mothers has in fact worsened in
the period between 1983 (when the previous census study of
Alimony and Child Support was published) and 1985. After
adjusting for inflation, the 1985 average child support
payment declined about 12%.below 1983 levels.[16]

Why are child support awards set so low, relative to need?

Judges in divorce cases are empowered to set the amounts
for alimony and child care. In some cases the judge is an
older male, perhaps out of touch with the realities of
sneakers out-grown or worn-out, broken or lost glasses;
sometimes humongous appetites. Whatever the reason, the
post-divorce distribution of the husband's income has usually
favored him over the ex-wife and children.

With such low dollar support from the ex-husband, and
regardless of the age of any children, the divorced mother
will have to make up, out of her "woman's job" earnings, the
difference between the child support payment and the actual
cost of raising the chlidren. Thus, it is not surprising
that divorced women are much more likely than married women

to be employed; three-quarters of all divorced women were in the labor force in 1987.[17] And if jobs are unavailable, or necessary child care is unavailable, the family has no recourse but to turn to public welfare support which is generally inadequate. In 1988, AFDC monthly welfare payments, combined with food stamps, left the recipient families below the poverty line in all states.[18]

AND that brings up the cost of paid child care. (The Department of Agriculture budget assumes that child care would be provided free by a non-working parent.) The cost of child care usually exceeds the typical child support award. In Colorado the cost of licensed day care was reported to be twice the amount of the average child support payment.[19]

A new day may have dawned with respect to getting ex-husbands to come through with the court-ordered support. In 1984, the federal Child Support Enforcement Act required states to take action against defaulters through payroll withholding, tax refund interceptions, wage attachments and other similar measures. The 1988 Family Security Act has supposedly tightened up the law, and enforcement procedures, though some provisions will not take effect until 1994. (Hang on, kiddies)

Until now, judges have been reluctant to embarrass otherwise law-abiding, middle-class citizens, sometimes with two families to support following the divorce. As husbands moved from state to state, collection became harder. As judges retired, or moved to different jurisdictions, the whole case sometimes moved back to Square One, while a new judge would give the defaulting husband an opportunity to make good. The situation became extremely frustrating for the mother, because of the difficulties with the court enforcement system,

The Los Angeles Times reported a 1988 case of a California mother of three girls who sent the two younger children to live with the father because:

"There was no way that we could live on my salary alone. My children are teenagers, and they understand that they're not able to get everything they want (if they live with her) My ex-husband is self-employed, and he made $1.4 million in 1985. From November of 1985 to the middle of 1988, I received $1300 in child support".[20]

Will the new laws work? States have been slow to pass laws to implement the federal requirements, and judges hesitant to enforce the law. Even if all payments are made in full, as noted above, the custodial mother is still going to be providing most of the support to the couple's children, not just in emotional terms, but in cold cash share. And if an older mother with minimum work experience cannot make it

financially, the family has no alternative except the welfare
rolls.

How you can cope with problems of divorce, alimony, child
support:

1.   LOOK BEFORE YOU LEAP - An abusive or stingy boyfriend,
or one addicted to alcohol or drugs, is probably not going to
undergo a miraculous transformation on his wedding day.

2.   If the marriage cannot be salvaged, get legal advice as
soon as possible.

3.   JOIN with other women to work for adequate levels of
child support, and/or alimony, and an equitable division of
marital property.

4.   JOIN with other voters to work for national health
insurance.

UNEMPLOYMENT:

   Although federal and state laws have been passed since the
1960's with the intent of moving women and minorities into
mainstream employment and better-paid-jobs, the sluggishness
of the American economy in the 1980's rolled back some of the
gains, under a "last hired, first fired" policy. Seniority is
generally accepted as a fair way to administer layoffs, but
because women had just begun to move into higher paid
occupations, the cutbacks have halted that progress. (What
is needed to help all workers, regardless of sex, race, or
any other characteristic is a strong government commitment
to a full employment policy -- that is, jobs should be
available for all who are willing and able to work.
Discussion of this important policy is beyond the scope of
this book, however.) But it is important to consider the
general situation of women with respect to unemployment.

THE PROBLEM: Women are more likely than men to be employed
               in low-paid jobs ; as a result, their average
               unemployment benefit in 1982 provided income
               below the poverty line for a single person,
               while the average benefit for men was above
               the poverty line for two persons.

               Married women whose family responsibilities
               result in intermittent employment may be
               ineligible for unemployment Compensation under
               some state rules.

   For many years, from the nineteen fifties on, female
workers usually had a higher unemployment rate than did male
workers; only in the 1980's did the male rate begin to rise
above the female rate, reflecting the depressed state of
employment in steel, auto, and other heavy industries where
employment is predominantly male. Also, with the growth of

the service industries in the 1980's, "temporary" and part-time employment became more prominent in the employment picture.

> Because women are more likely than men to be employed as part-time or temporary employees in small business, light manufacturing or the service sector, they are more likely to experience repeated spells of unemployment. But it is women's family situation which explains much of women's unemployment pattern. Before and after children are born, or whenever they need care at home, it is more likely to be mothers than fathers who leave work; the father's paycheck is generally larger, and therefore cannot be sacrificed. Then when women try to re-enter the labor force, there may be difficulties and delays in once more finding employment.

In small firms, with less than 15 employees, protection of pregnancy disability is not covered under Title VII of the Civil Rights Act. As a result, a woman leaving her job for childbirth is not guaranteed under federal law the right to return to her job; some states have required such protection. Even if a woman has return rights, she may choose to remain at home for a longer period, or may be forced to remain out of the work force if no child care is available. In either case, when she decides to return to work, she will usually have to spend some time searching for a job, and thus experience a period of unemployment.

Although most states permit a woman to receive unemployment benefits if she is denied reinstatement after taking maternity leave, Missouri, Minnesota, North Dakota, Vermont and the District of Columbia disqualify anyone from collecting unemployment benefits for leaving work because of a non-job-related reason. In 1987, the U. S. Supreme Court ruled: "If a state adopts a neutral rule that incidentally disqualifies pregnant or formerly pregnant claimants as part of a larger group, the neutral application of that rule" is legal.[21] This argument is reminiscent of the earlier Supreme Court decision upholding the denial of company-provided sick leave benefits to pregnant women; the Court held that there was no discrimination in that case, because if men became pregnant, they would also be denied benefits. The resulting furore led the U. S. Congress to pass the Pregnancy Discrimination Act in 1978, which requires that companies which provide sick leave and disability benefits to workers include pregnancy under that coverage.

Again, it is important for you to check YOUR OWN STATE LAWS. Unemployment Compensation regulations are set by each state (within some basic federal guidelines). Even in the years when the unemployment rate for women was consistently higher than that for men, women were less likely than men to

receive Unemployment Compensation. In some states, because
of their low earnings, women are ineligible for benefits.
Eligibility standards are set by each state, and may call for
some minimum level of annual earnings, or at least two
quarters of coverage in the preceding year. Even when a
woman worker has met the eligibility requirements, she may be
denied benefits if she quits for a non-work-related reason
(to care for a sick child, for instance). Although there are
exceptions allowed for "domestic quits," unless a worker is a
"major, or sole support" of the family, benefits can be
denied. Thus a married woman, with husband present, could be
denied an exception which would be granted to a male
breadwinner in the same situation.[22]

A woman who works part-time because of child-care
arrangements will usually be unable to collect Unemployment
Compensation, even if her company goes out of business,
unless she is "available" for full-time work. (All claimants
must be able and willing to work at suitable offered jobs.)

Because Unemployment Compensation is related to earning
levels, those women who do collect receive on average lower
benefits than male unemployed; they are more likely than men
to be denied benefits. For an unemployed woman who is a
single parent, even if child support payments are made, there
may be no alternative to accepting Public Welfare assistance.

How you can cope with Unemployment Compensation
disadvantages for women:

1. JOIN WITH OTHER WOMEN to urge your state representatives
to amend the state laws with respect to eligibility for
Unemployment Compensation to recognize the problems of women.
(Other industrialized countries have programs to support
single mothers, or intact families with low income when the
mother is required to remain at home by family needs.)

It is understandable that employers, particularly
struggling owners of small business, strongly resist any
increase in their contributions to the Unemployment Insurance
Fund. Women's groups, however, may enlist business support
for national legislation to provide FAMILY INCOME in order to
permit parents to remain at home with small children if that
is the choice.

2. When possible, do not be too quick to take a part-time, or
"temp" job which will leave you without earned income, and
often without Unemployment Compensation, when it ends.

GET THE NECESSARY TRAINING OR EDUCATION which will give you
job opportunities in the Primary Labor Market - that is,
full-time, full-year employment, with a good salary and
necessary fringe benefits - health, disability and life
insurance as well as pension coverage.

.If you have to take a less desirable job, keep your eyes and ears open for better prospects elsewhere, and either persuade your employer to match bids from other employers, or go where the grass is greener.

Although you should not change jobs every week, you should ALWAYS BE IN THE LABOR MARKET.

MILITARY AND CIVIL SERVICE

There is one employment area where state and federal governments could take direct action to improve the employment status of women--that is in the military and the civil service:

THE PROBLEM: Because women have not been recruited in equal numbers with men into the armed forces, fewer women than men have veterans' status. As a result, women are at a disadvantage in the scoring of Civil Service examinations, and thus in opportunities for employment, and for promotion to executive positions.

Within the military service, women have been denied equal opportunity for more challenging and better-paid assignments.

Women in the past have been excluded from the military draft, and even in 1990 are restricted by Congressional ceilings on the number of women admitted to the services, and by exclusion from "combat" positions. They have further been excluded, because of height or other restrictions, from certain military jobs necessary for career advancement. We all probably would agree that those men and women who have suffered through the miseries and dangers of wartime combat, at low military pay levels, should be compensated by the public they have protected. There are in fact many government programs which provide educational assistance, home loan guarantees, disability compensation, and social security credit for returning veterans.

Yet because women have been excluded by law from the opportunity to serve their country in the military, they also have suffered disadvantage in obtaining government employment and promotions. One state law gives _absolute preference_ to any veteran scoring a passing grade on a Civil Service exam, and this arrangement was upheld by the U.S. Supreme Court;[23] other states and the federal government award additional points to veterans' test scores, for hiring and promotion. As a result of this system, men predominate in the high-paid civil service positions, while women are the great majority of the lower ranks.(See Appendix Table A-2)

Some women may see an advantage in the tradeoff, and would prefer restricted job opportunity to entering the armed forces in time of war. Yet civilians in any future war are likely to suffer more casualties than the better-protected service personnel. Women are doubly penalized for being "protected" against military service, with a lifetime of low pay capped by an old age on an inadequate pension.

For those women who today try to enter the services, there are many career stumbling blocks. Marine Corps rules set higher education and intelligence levels for women recruits than for men;[24] the Army, according to the Congressional Caucus for Women's Issues, has not assigned women to jobs for which they were trained, and thus has limited their promotion opportunities;[25] the Navy was successfully challenged by the Women's Equity Action League on its attempt to establish "anthropometric entrance standards" (Pentagonese for a pilot's reach, including leg, hip and thigh measurements.)[26] "Such standards would have prevented most interested Navy women from entering flight training and also affected large numbers of Hispanic and Asian men in the Navy who typically are smaller in stature than Anglo males."[27]

In another WEAL case, submarine engineer technician, Pamella Doviak was barred by Navy policy from sea duty aboard a submarine; in order to get a promotion, sea duty is required. After the WEAL investigators requested documents under the Freedom of Information Act, they "received dozens of documents confirming that women in shipyards all around the country are being denied access to sea trial assignments on submarines." [28] (The Navy argument asserted that the addition of a women would "unacceptably degrade crew habitability", yet, as witness Sally Ride, "Accommodations aren't an issue for women astronauts".) What is really the problem is the human resistance to newcomers encroaching on established turf. In city halls, police and fire stations around the country, the problem persists, and each aspiring woman in turn has been required to fight her own battle for equal employment opportunity.

The whole range of discrimination by the military is slowly being modified; in December 1987 Secretary of the Navy Webb issued a redefinition of "combat" which could open up 15,000 jobs to women. He acted after the Defense Advisory Committee on Women in the services reported that "women in the Navy and Marine Corps deployed in the Pacific region were frequently the victims of sexual harassment and abuse and appeared to be locked in dead-end jobs that offered few chances of advancement."[29]

How you can cope with obstacles to a career in the military and Civil Service.

If you want educational opportunities you can't afford, or have an urge to travel and see the world, look up your local military recruiter. But be sure to FIND OUT what are the opportunities that will be available for you--skill training, educational benefits, opportunities for promotion. Send a male friend as well, to compare options for the sexes. (He doesn't have to actually sign up, unless he chooses to!)

JOIN with other voters to urge an end to ceilings on voluntary enlistment by women in the armed services.

USE the Federal Equal Employment Opportunity Commission, and your own state Commission Against Discrimination to assist you in obtaining Civil Service employment or promotion if you have reason to believe you are being discriminated against only because of your sex (or race, religion, or ethnic origin).(See Appendix B and E for list of useful agencies, public and private.)

The Criminal Justice System

The American legal system may fairly be characterized as predominantly male--judges, lawyers, administrators, court officers. Study panels in New York, New Jersey and Rhode Island, set up to determine whether state courts were biased against women, have documented complaints of discrimination against female lawyers, witnesses and litigants. The New York study of the state justice system found the bias against women so widespread that "they are often denied equal justice." [30] This lack of representation for women can adversely affect a woman's chances for favorable resolution of civil cases (for example, in the divorce, as noted earlier in this chapter) but there is also a possibility of bias in criminal proceedings.

It is not possible in this brief account (nor within the competence of this writer) to discuss the entire legal system of the United States. The complexity of the criminal justice system defies brief summation; there are parallel systems with separate or shared jurisdiction over certain types of illegal behavior, administered by the federal government, or by state, city or county. This chapter will look only at some key areas where there is evidence that females are treated differently from males, and consider the impact of these differences on the lives of women.

Punishment under the criminal justice system:

THE PROBLEM: Many imprisoned women are confined for offenses related to sexual activity or prostitution; men are rarely imprisoned for their participation in commercial sex.

    Fewer tax dollars are allotted to women prisoners as compared to men, to provide skill training for their re-entry into society.

Part of the problem of discussing "equal justice" for women offenders is that women are only a small part of the prison population. In 1985, there were almost half a million male prisoners in state and federal institutions compared to less than 25,000 female prisoners;[31] although women are over half the U.S. population, they represent less than 5% of such prisoners. Some observers may believe that such a statistic indicates that chivalry is at work, and that women may be excused where men would be prosecuted, or in general be more leniently treated by the criminal justice system; there is no objective evidence to support this view. It is estimated that 30 to 50% of all incarcerated girls and women have been imprisoned for activities connected with prostitution. [32] Although it takes two to tango, any penalties for commercial sex activity imposed by the local authorities or the state courts, are applied almost exclusively to women; the male "customer" is rarely imprisoned.

It is also suggested that women in prison are treated better than male counterparts. Women's penal institutions often have more of a "dormitory" life style, presumably because women are less likely to act violently, and thus require less restraint. Whether imprisonment can ever be made pleasant is debatable, but in terms of appropriations for recreational and job training facilities, women are usually on the short end of appropriations, on a per capita basis. While some imprisoned men are given the opportunity in machine shops or automobile repair programs to learn better-paying skills, women are given "training" designed to funnel them into the lowest-paying jobs of our society: household worker, beautician, stitcher - traditional "women's jobs".

Thus when a prostitute is released, her job options are limited, not only by the fact of a criminal record, but by her lack of skills. She can find employment only in the same low-paid occupations which made prostitution financially attractive in the first place. As mentioned in Chapter Two, a retail sales weekly paycheck is totally inadequate for women supporting children; and in all 50 states, the total AFDC (Welfare) benefits plus food stamps add up to an income below the poverty line.

When a woman is imprisoned, she and any children she may have are more likely to suffer from the separation. There is no "wife" to keep the family intact, as is usually the case for male prisoners who are fathers. Women's prisons are often located in rural areas where family visits are difficult to arrange. Perhaps she should have thought of that, is the response of the righteous--but still a problem for women who run afoul of the law in their struggle for economic survival.

Among younger women offenders, girls have tended to serve longer sentences than boys. "The majority of girls are confined for running away from home, sexual activity, or having a child", while the majority of boys are confined for

offences such as larceny or breaking and entering.
Connecticut makes it a crime to be.."an unmarried girl
between 16 and 21 who is 'in manifest danger of falling into
habits of vice'. If girls run away from home, disobey their
parents, have a child without marrying or are promiscuous,
they are branded as 'juvenile delinquents'. Boys engaged in
the same conduct are seldom even referred to the juvenile
court.'[33]

How you can cope with the criminal justice system:

Stay out of it.

Get training or education while you are young so that
you can support yourself, and any children you may have. If
your children are young, and child care is unavailable, get
temporary help from AFDC, and community service
organizations.

Protection by the Justice System

THE PROBLEM: Assault by a stranger is a crime more surely and
severely punished than is assault by a husband
on his wife.

A rape victim is often blamed for the crime.

Let us now look at the other side of the coin. We have
seen that women are more likely than men to be imprisoned for
illegal sexual behavior. When they are imprisoned, fewer
state dollars are likely to be spent on giving them adequate
recreational opportunities, or training facilities to prepare
them for life after imprisonment. So chivalry is not very
much in evidence when it comes to women's offences against
the law. But how about protection of women against law-

breakers specifically against abusive husbands, boy friends,
lovers, or a rapist.

Domestic Violence

As recorded almost daily in the news media, violence is a
way of life for many women. The criminal justice system does
not punish abusive husbands as it attempts to punish those
convicted of violence against strangers.

A few examples (from Massachusetts newspapers)--- papers in
your own state very likely have similar stories:

The Massachusetts legislature passed in 1978 an Abuse
Prevention Act entitling abused wives to civil protection
against violence by spouses.(in recognition of the reluctance
of many women to file criminal charges against their
children's father and often essential family provider.) Yet
when a battered Massachusetts woman sought a district court
order barring the husband temporarily from their home to
ensure her safety, the judge suggested that she file a
criminal complaint. He commented; "There is no quick fix in
the Dorchester Court. ...If I see visible signs that a
woman's been beaten up, I'll put him out for a few days. I
do it very seldom. I don't believe in breaking up families.[34]

Another District Court Judge granted the battered wife's
request for a restraining order against her husband, but
denied her plea for police protection "and castigated her in
open court for wasting his time and the taxpayer's money."
Shortly afterward, while the wife was waiting at a bus stop
with her mother, the estranged husband forced her into his
car. She was 22 and pregnant when she was killed and her
body discarded at the Lexington dump.'[35]

Another Massachusetts woman complained to the Chief Justice
about verbal abuse by the judge in her case, "that he should
blame me for causing the court trouble when it was my
husband who was on trial is abominable." The Chief Justice
rejected her complaint, replying that she had failed to
appear in court on the appointed day, and had caused a great
deal of inconvenience to the court. However, according to
those present, she was in court that day; the only time the
woman left the courtroom was when she was ordered out by
court personnel because her baby was crying.[36]

Domestic violence affects families across the racial and
economic spectrum. Battered women in middle-class
circumstances may have even greater trouble in obtaining
relief. According to social worker Susan Manatt, "an abused
black woman who lived in a nice home in an upper class
neighborhood was told by a probate court judge that she and
her husband were one of the black couples who had made it,
and he didn't want to break up their family. The judge tried
to persuade her to go back to her abusive husband and refused
to order him to vacate their home."[37]

In one very well-publicized case, a top official in the
federal Securities and Exchange Commission repeatedly beat
his wife during their marriage, even when she was pregnant.
He was forced to resign his prestigious post when the case
received publicity after she finally went to court for
protection.[38]

This book does not attempt to address the causes of
violence by husband and father. Sometimes the abuser was
himself abused as a child. Certainly job pressures, and
especially periods ot unemployment, can be related to a rise
in reported abuse of spouse and children. The male
breadwinner who cannot take the risk of changing an
intolerable work situation because he is the major family
support is likely to vent his frustration at home.

Local police are reluctant to respond as they would in the
case of assault by a stranger. Perhaps the couple will
resolve their differences; the man may have been a good
provider; what will the family do without his income? Yet,
domestic violence may feed on itself, and unless police
intervene, the ultimate charge may be murder.

How you can cope with domestic violence.

If you are abused, immediately seek help from the police
and the courts. Although these agencies in the past have
often "blamed the victim," in recent years there has been a
growing sensitivity to the problems of battered women. In
1986,the U.S. Department of Justice issued a
report"Confronting Domestic Violence: A Guide for Criminal
Justice Agencies," and suggested appropriate ways for police
to respond to complaints. A District Attorney in
Massachusetts responded to a series of articles in the Boston
Globe on battered women, proposing that "attention be focused
on the many more women who tragically endure years of abuse
in silence. These are the women we must reach and urge to
report by repeatedly explaining to them that no person should
have to live in fear of harm at the hands of a husband or
male companion, and that there are agencies and organizations
which offer assistance and support."[39]

Many abusive individuals were themselves abused as
children, and need help. The woman cited above who
complained to the Massachusetts Chief Justice wrote; "My
filing the complaint and the court having issued the
complaint was the first time anyone had ever held my husband
accountable for his violent behavior. The impending threat
of jail or probation and public embarrassment was the impetus
that caused my husband to seek help." (Her husband continued
to receive treatment and the abuse stopped.)[40]

If your spouse cannot change his behavior, there are shelters for battered women and their families in most cities. It is no disgrace to have chosen an unsuitable mate, but it is foolish and sometimes fatal to continue to endure abuse.

Rape

THE PROBLEM; When a woman brings a complaint of rape to the police, she often finds that there is a mindset which includes two basic assumptions:
"The woman will usually lie" and
"the woman really consented, so it wasn't rape."[41]

A woman's past sexual experiences, her style of dress, or her way of spending an evening out may be used to discredit her testimony. In the past decade there have been reforms in the laws of some states, and in federal law, relating to evidence in rape cases. Yet because the police and court systems continue to be male dominated, the woman victim is still likely to be subjected to humiliating questions by police, or in court by defendant's lawyer.

How you can cope with rape:

When you report the crime (which you should do immediately, if possible) bring a supportive friend to the police station, who will be better able to defend you against suggestive questioning. You do not have to answer questions about your past sex life. Your friend should also accompany you to the police doctor or hospital; you may also want to go to your own doctor for treatment and an anti-pregnancy pill.[42]

JOIN WITH OTHER WOMEN and organized women's groups to abolish special rules in rape cases. Also, it may be desirable to seek lower penalties for rapists, because there is reluctance by courts to impose life sentences for the act of rape; this would also increase the possibility for convictions. In only a few states (Oregon, New Jersey, Iowa and Delaware) are wives protected against sexual assault by their husband; elsewhere, women should seek to outlaw spousal rape.

Retirement Income: Social Security and Private Pensions

> "Old Mother Hubbard
> Went to the cupboard
> To get her poor doggie a bone
> But when she got there
> The cupboard was bare
> And so her poor doggie had none."

That's a dog's life for you. Say, have you ever wondered what the good mother was eating for supper that night?

THE PROBLEM: Women past their child-bearing lives are
begrudged a decent standard of living by
society.

Poverty among older women is nothing new. In the bible story, the widow Ruth was struggling to provide food not only for herself, but for her mother-in-law, Naomi. To a teenager, thinking about economic survival after age 60 is JUST BORING! But the millions of poor women in their sixties and seventies were all teenagers once. What happened along the way?

Some women, married or single, work all their adult lives, but many married women have only intermittent employment in the period when they are bearing children and for some years thereafter. If women are not willing to take this time out of the paid labor force, society could not renew itself-- Adios, America. Yet although motherhood is given lip service, society appears to penalize rather than to reward married women as they grow older.

Social Security

> "Congress may or may not ultimately
> decide that earnings sharing is the
> appropriate way to reform Social Security
> But one thing is certain: we must find a way
> to reform the system to assure older women a
> decent standard of living. That's the
> unfinished business of Social Security."
>
> Dr. Arthur Flemming, former
> Secretary of U.S. Department of
> Health, Education and Welfare.

The Social Security system was begun during the depression of the nineteen-thirties to relieve the abject poverty of millions of elderly Americans who had worked all their lives, but found themselves desperately poor at life's close. Under this system, in a period when few married women worked outside the home, the retirement benefits earned by the husband over his working life would be increased by one-half for a living spouse, (and additional funds if there were other dependents.) For example, if a man's lifetime earnings would entitle him at age 65 to a monthly Social Security retirement benefit of $800, an additional $400 would be provided for the spouse, so that a couple could share a $1200 monthly income after the husband's retirement.

Today, most women, married or single, are likely to be working for much of their lives. The Social Security program taxes each worker, and his or her employer, a certain percentage of earnings. At the time of retirement, a worker's contributions are totalled, and monthly benefits for the rest of life are paid to retirees. No distinction is made in the tax as to whether the worker is male or female, married, single, divorced or widowed; anyone working in covered employment pays the tax, and his or her employer matches that contribution to the Social Security Fund. (Currently over 7.5% each, for employer and employee.)

When a man reaches age 65 (or 62 if he chooses to accept reduced benefits) he may file for Social Security benefits. His monthly benefit will be increased by 50% for a spouse. Even if the wife has worked her entire married life, and even if she has had no children, it is likely that her own benefits, based on her own earnings, would be less than 50% of her husband's benefits, because she has usually worked in low-paid women's jobs.

Common sense indicates that the couple will prefer to receive the larger sum, that is, a 50% increase in the husband's benefit, and the wife will forfeit the benefits she would be entitled on her own account. The advantage of taking a half share of the husband's benefit, rather than the wife's own benefit, is even greater when the wife has had many years out of the labor force while her children were being born, and during their young years; in that case she will have had many "Zero" years of contribution to be figured in her own benefit.(like the "zero"boxes in your bowling string -- it sure drags it down')

But then, why has the married woman contributed a percentage of her wages throughout her working years, if she is to receive no return on those SS contributions in her older years? The implied answer is that she is getting the 50% of her husband's benefit which she has not "earned." (Try that explanation on a wife and mother of your acquaintance.) The wife and mother who chose to remain at home during all her married life would receive the same 50% of her husband's benefit. Essentially, the contributions of the millions of married working women who will never collect on their own accounts have bolstered the Social Security Fund and staved off fears of a bankrupt system. (SEE Appendix G.)

As a woman in Indiana wrote to her Senator:

> "In two years, I will retire and I have two
> options. Take half my husband's Social Security
> or all of my own. In either case, I lose and the
> government gets a fat and free donation from my
> years of labor both inside and outside the
> home.[43]

About one third of all retiring women workers now face this
Hobson's choice.

Because the combined employer and employee contributions
are now about 15% of annual earnings, a woman's substantial
lifetime "savings" simply vanish under the present system.
"Earnings sharing" has been proposed as a fair way to resolve
this problem of married women who are forced to forfeit their
Social Security contributions in this way. Under "earnings
sharing", the Social Security earnings credits of husband and
wife would be combined during marriage, and divided into two
individual records when calculating retirement benefits. To
each partner's record would be added the individual credits
earned prior to marriage and following divorce or widowhood.
(Divorce and the possible creation of a new family entitled
to a share of Social Security benefits may further erode a
former wife's share). Even though women are more than half
the voters, *they have not let their male Senators and
Representatives know* that they <u>want the Social Security
System reformed in order to prevent millions of women from
ending their lives in poverty</u>. A 1990 report by the Older
Women"s League "Heading for Hardship: Retirement Income for
American Women In the Next Century" (730 Eleventh Street, NW,
Suite 300, Washington, D.C.20001) documents the bleak future
awaiting many women at the end of their lives.

Another problem affecting women under the Social Security
System is described as "the widow's gap." In contrast to
other (non-disabled) workers, widows can begin to collect
Social Security benefits as early as age 60. But the woman
who becomes widowed at age 53, and whose youngest child is 16
years of age, must wait until she is 60 to begin to receive
benefits. A woman who has spent her life in homemaking and
child-raising is often not prepared to re-enter the labor
force; her skills are rusty; her self-confidence is low.
Even when she gets up her courage to seek employment, she
often finds that employers prefer the "bright eyes and nimble
fingers" of younger workers.

The average Social Security monthly benefit for retired
workers 65 and over in 1983 was $371 for women, and $478 for
men.[44]

Private Pensions:

Although married women are at a disadvantage in the Social Security public pension system, almost **all** women are disadvantaged under the _private_ pension system. Only the larger employers are likely to provide private pensions for workers; male workers predominate in the heavy industry (steel, autos) where union-negotiated pensions are most likely to be provided. Where women predominate in employment (insurance, chain retailers) the practice has often been to "integrate" private pensions and Social Security, so that increases in Social Security benefits will be to some extent offset by a decrease in the private pension payments. Pension integration affects low-paid workers more than high-paid workers; because private pensions are based on wages as well as years with the company, the small pension might be partly canceled or completely wiped out. The amount of "integration" permitted has been cut back by the 1986 Economic Equity Act; now workers are eligible to receive one-half their earned pension before the "integration" can be figured in. This change helps - - but not very much. The same act also lowered "vesting" time from ten years to five.

Despite these improvements, it is still the case that many fewer women receive private pensions as compared to men, and their pensions are much smaller. In 1985 only 37% of women received private pensions, compared to 48% of men; almost three times as many men were recorded in the top earnings bracket, where pension coverage is most likely, and pensions larger.[45] Because women have such low monthly income from Social Security, and have low or non-existent private pensions, in their old age many become dependent on public assistance (SSI). Women are three-fourths of the aged receiving Supplementary Security Income.[46] Potential Bag Ladies can begin lining up right here.

How you can cope with the pension system and provide better for old age:

____The best way to cope is to prepare yourself for a well-paid job at the top of the Social Security earnings base, in order that Social Security benefits on your own account will be larger than 50% of your husband's benefit. Prepare yourself for better-paying employment by taking appropriate skills-training or academic programs. When job-hunting, compare the possible employers with respect to their pension programs for employees. (Industries with strong unions tend to offer better pensions.)

JOIN with other women to urge legislators to enact new
Social Security regulations which will set up "Earnings
Sharing"; that is, each partner in a marriage will be
credited with half the couple's total earnings so that if
widowhood or divorce occurs, the wife will have an earnings
base to build on.

Summary

"The System" does not provide equal justice for women in
many areas besides those noted in this chapter. Some of
these injustices are not well recognized either by the males
who dominate the system, or by women themselves.

Overall, the best way to bring about change is for women to
participate more fully in the legal and governmental
institutions of American society. If more women aspire to
become lawyers, the likely result would be more women serving
as judges. If more women ran for office at the state and
federal level, they would be in a position - as
Representatives or Senators - to protect the rights of women
and children.

"If you want anything done, the best way is to do it
yourself."

70

[1] Lenore J. Weitzman, <u>The Divorce Revolution,</u> (New York: The Free Press, 1985, pp.106-108. (Hereafter cited as <u>Weitzman</u>)

[2] National Council of Negro Women, Inc. <u>Women and Housing:</u> A report on sex discrimination in 5 American Cities. (Atlanta, St. Louis, San Antonio, San Francisco, Washington, D.C.) U. S. Department of Housing and Urban Development,Washington, D.C. (U.S. Government Printing Office, 1975) Testimony of Attorney Emily J. Goodman, New York City Hearing, p.37.

[3] 1988 <u>Statistical Abstract</u>, Table 435.

[4] In re Marriage of Brantner 67 Cal. App.3d 416, 419,420,136 Cal Rptr. 635 (1977)Quoted in <u>Weitzman,</u> p.194.

[5] U. S. Department of Commerce, Bureau of the Census, "Child Support and Alimony,1985". Advance data from March-April 1986 Current Population Reports, Series P-23-152, Table 1, p.8. (Hereafter cited as <u>1985 Child Support and Alimony.)</u>

[6] <u>Weitzman,</u> p.192

[7] 1985 <u>Child Support and Alimony,</u> Table 1, p.8.

[8] 1985 <u>Child Support and Alimony</u>, Table 1, p.8

[9] In re Marriage of Brantner (op cit.); quoted in Weitzman, pp.193-94.

[10] Judith Gaines, "Reforming the Nation's Child Support Laws". In <u>Boston Globe</u>, December 25, 1988.

[11] National Conference of State Legislatures, "The Effects of Non Support", Information Release #9, 1983.(Quoted in "The Myth of Equality", NOW LDEF, 99 Hudson Street, NY, 10013.)

[12] 1985 <u>Child Support and Alimony,</u> Table A, p.1; p.3.

[13] <u>Ibid.,</u> Table D, p.4

[14] U.S. Department of Agriculture,"Updated Estimates of the Cost of Raising a Child," <u>Family Economics Review,</u> 1988, Vol. 2, pp. 36-37. (Fifty percent adjustment for second child based on method of Thomas Espenshade, quoted in <u>Weitzman, p.271</u>.)

[15] 1985 <u>Child Support and Alimony</u>, Table D, p.4

[16] <u>Ibid</u>., Table D p.4

[17] 1988 <u>Statistical Abstract</u>, Table 624, p.374.

[18] Center on Social Welfare Policies and Law "Analysis of 1988 Benefit Levels in the Program of Aid to Families with Dependent Children", 1019 Vermont Avenue, N.W. Washington, D.C. 20005-33592; 95 Madison Avenue, New York, 10016-7842; March, 1988, p.1.

[19] "Effects of Non Support" (1983)

[20] Lori Silver, "Full Child Support; Small Steps" <u>Los Angeles Times,</u> 1/23/89, pp.1:12.

[21] <u>San Diego Union</u>, 1/22/87, p.A 1.

[22] Diana Pearce, "Toil and Trouble: Women Workers and Unemploymeent Compensation", SIGNS, Spring 1985, p.456.

[23] WEAL Washington Report, Vol. 6 No.5, October 1977, p.1.

[24] <u>Boston Globe</u>, 4/26/88

[25] <u>Baltimore Sun</u>, 12/28/81; Congressional Caucus for Women's Issues, 9/30/87.

[26] WEAL Washington Report, October-November 1984; August-September 1986.

[27] WEAL Washington Report, August-September 1986, p.7.

[28] WEAL Washington Report, October–November 1985..

[29] Boston Globe, 12/22/87

[30] Boston Globe, 12/19/86

[31] 1988 Statistical Abstract, Table 306, p.175.

[32] Feinman, C. Women in Criminal Justice. New York: Praeger Publishers, 1980., p.25.

[33] S.Ross and A. Barcher. Rights of Women: the Basic ACLU Guide to a Woman's Rights. New York: Sunrise Books, 1973. pp.152–53.

[34] Boston Globe, 11//13/86

[35] Ibid., 9/21/86

[36] Ibid., 9/27/86

[37] Ibid , 12/10/87, p.55

[38] Ibid., 9/17/87; 12/12/87.

[39] Boston Globe Letter from Scott Harshbarger, District Attorney of Middlesex County, 11/13/88.

[40] Boston Globe, 9/27/86

[41] Ross and Barcher, Rights of Women, pp.163–74.

[42] Susan Estrich, Real Rape. Cambridge, MA: Harvard University Press, 1987.

[43] OWL Observer, March–April 1987

[44] Denton R. Vaughan, "Development and Evaluation of a Survey-Baased Type Benefit Classification for the Social Security Program"., Social Security Bulletin, January 1989,pp.188–19, Tables 5 and 6.

[45] 1988 Statistical Abstract, p.344, Table 568.

[46] Social Security Bulletin, January 1984, Vol.47 (1) Chart 1, p.17.

CHAPTER VI

REVIEWING THE TRIP

"Hey, man—lighten up."

Drawing by Ed Fisher c 1989
The New Yorker Magazine, Inc.

Looking back - it's a pretty bumpy road. How gloomy can
you get? Is that all there is?

No way. To be human is to experience joys and sorrows
throughout life. Only a poet can express the feelings of men
and women as you share these joys and sorrows with
families,friends, and lovers. This book is intended only to
help young women recognize the preventable hazards that lie
on the way ahead, around the corner. If a woman is to
appreciate the joys of life, to take time to smell the roses,
she must survive in economic terms; as well, to have the
strength to bear life's sorrows, women must be able to keep
their heads above water.

This is not to say that life is a bed of roses for men.
All young people, men and women, face the problem of breaking
into the labor market. But for young women, the problem is
compounded by the barriers noted in the preceding chapters.
Women do not usually have the resources available to young
men - a tradition or network of older relatives and friends
who are able to point out the routes to valuable skills, to
better-paying jobs, to union membership. So your first goal
should be to equip yourself with marketable skills.

USE the offices of your high school or college Guidance
Counsellors, and check with the school librarians for the
printed materials they can supply, to give you an idea of the
range of job possibilities. DON'T SETTLE **for the same old
low-paying jobs** where women are becoming ever more
concentrated!

Look at the U.S. Department of Labor <u>Occupational Outlook
Handbook</u> for job descriptions and typical pay scales; compare
the earnings of various occupations in the Labor Department
publications, especially the <u>Monthly Labor Review,</u> or
<u>Employment and Earnings.</u>.

Having a marketable skill in a good paying field is
essential to economic survival. In the South Sea islands. it
may be possible to survive if you have the ability to knock
down coconuts, but in an urban, industrial society, you must
trade your skills for bread,(and butter),(and something to
wear), (and a place to live), (and a car)....The skills you
learn in your shop classes, or public vocational school, or
college classes won't last a lifetime - but they will give
you a base to build on.

Technology keeps changing, and you will probably need
several "retreads" over a lifetime. But if you start out
equipped with some specialized skill, it is easier to update
or transform it. The satisfaction you obtain from mastering
a skill is great for your self esteem (way better than even
liposuction! or whatever!) - AND gives you a fair chance to
earn a livable income.

Invade the shop classes - it's fun! Check with labor
unions to find out about possible apprenticeships. For those
young women who have enjoyed Mathematics, Biology, Chemistry,
or Physics, consider a career in Science, Medicine, or
Engineering. A career as a physician would help other women
and their families; that is, a woman physician may be less
likely to perform unnecessary operations, and more willing to
suggest remedies for overworked wives and mothers other than
prescription drugs.

Young women are needed in politics, to monitor the way
the political system handles the problems affecting women's
lives: alimony and child support, and the division of marital
property and income following divorce; protection against
violence; provision of public funds for day care and
national health insurance, as well as family leave
legislation; women's access to education and job
opportunities; the funds allotted for job training for women
prisoners; the regulations which limit unemployment
compensation for women; the Congressional and military
restrictions on employment of women in the armed forces, and
the related restrictions on women civil servants who are kept
at the bottom of the totem pole; protection of women
consumers against discriminatory prices by insurers or other
businesses; the Social Security regulations which deny women
in their old age a return on their contributions as workers
over their lifetime.

Political input by women, (and men), as parents and
voters, is also needed to improve the welfare of the nation's
children. Having children brings a multitude of joys, but to
keep those children well-fed, well-clothed, and well-housed
today usually requires the income of two working parents.
Because real wages (corrected for the shrinking value of the
dollar) have been declining steadily in recent years, young
couples often cannot duplicate the level of living they
experienced in their parents' homes. Often a wife's job is
essential to keep the family above the poverty level.

Depending on your economic status and job availability,
you may be able to combine work and child care. But with
newborns it may not be possible, and the resulting economic
pressures may affect your family's stability. For the single
mother, lack of child care may prevent job-holding, and force
a reliance on public welfare benefits. If you're in that
situation, get together with other young parents, and as
voters pressure the political system to recognize the need
for publicly-funded child care.

In the area of credit and housing availability, women in
general, and the single mother in particular, have been
disadvantaged. In spite of the laws at state and federal
levels, women have been restricted in their access to housing
by customary practices. Your economic status, and that of
your children, depends on the availability of decent,
affordable housing. If you want to be your own boss, the
chance of owning your own business depends on access to
credit. More political clout would help women achieve equal
access to credit and housing.

In this connection, an older woman who had been a state legislator for many years once told an audience of young Law School wives that they should consider going into politics. One of the young women in the audience politely expressed her doubts: "But Mrs. Smith, how do you know we are qualified?" Her answer: "Have you ever seen the State Legislature in session?"

Rome wasn't built in a day, so they say, and the entry of women into the political scene is not likely to change our country overnight. But today, with women the majority of eligible voters, there is a greater opportunity for women candidates to get elected to office and MAKE A DIFFERENCE!

So - Go for it!

Table A-1

1981
Female-male pay and
employment ratios

Occupational work level	Average monthly salary[1]	Female-male pay relationship[2]	Female share of total employment
Professional:			
Accountant I	$1.377	99	46
Accountant II	1.679	98	34
Accountant III	1.962	96	19
Accountant IV	2.402	95	11
Accountant V	2.928	90	5
Auditor I	1.364	98	36
Auditor II	1.651	97	27
Auditor III	2.033	92	21
Auditor IV	2.456	90	8
Attorney I	1.873	103	28
Attorney II	2.338	99	24
Attorney III	3.031	95	13
Attorney IV	3.738	94	9
Chemist I	1.508	96	38
Chemist II	1.757	94	29
Chemist III	2.120	93	15
Chemist IV	2.567	92	10
Administrative:			
Buyer I	1.350	96	52
Buyer II	1.689	95	23
Buyer III	2.100	92	9
Director of personnel I	2.321	101	21
Director of personnel II	2.933	94	10
Director of personnel III	3.574	90	7
Job analyst I	1.412	87	75
Job analyst II	1.525	92	85
Job analyst III	1.900	90	66
Job analyst IV	2.393	94	29
Technical:			
Engineering technician I	1.137	97	24
Engineering technician II	1.307	98	17
Engineering technician III	1.527	97	9
Drafter I	923	103	34
Drafter II	1.075	101	26
Drafter III	1.301	96	18
Drafter IV	1.611	94	8
Computer operator I	906	99	37
Computer operator II	1.049	102	49
Computer operator III	1.220	97	35
Computer operator IV	1.475	97	24
Computer operator V	1.733	92	17
Photographer II	1.425	96	6
Photographer III	1.704	106	5
Clerical:			
Accounting clerk I	798	94	95
Accounting clerk II	953	89	94
Accounting clerk III	1.121	89	91
Accounting clerk IV	1.407	84	82
Purchasing assistant I	1.002	93	95
Purchasing assistant II	1.278	87	84
Messenger	783	101	46

[1]Includes data for workers not identified by sex.

[2]Includes data only for workers identified by sex

SOURCE: Table reproduced from Mark S. Sieling "Staffing Patterns prominent in female-male earnings gap". <u>Monthly Labor Review</u>, June 1984, p.30, Table 2.

Table A-2

Civilian employees in the Federal Civil Service and Salary by Grade and Sex (September 1988)

Grade	Average * Salary	Total Employed	Women Employed	Women as Percent of Employed
01	$10,054	6,255	4,696	75 %
02	11,576	16,792	11,991	71
03	13,139	71,557	52,903	74
04	15,115	172,407	131,746	76
05	17,178	215,092	155,221	72
06	19,411	101,956	78,162	77
07	21,181	155,423	95,132	61
08	24,102	33,827	19,600	58
09	25,728	172,189	79,669	46
10	29,368	30,139	14,485	48
11	31,379	212,102	79,681	38
12	37,956	203,468	52,878	26
13	45,592	133,032	24,547	18
14	54,266	72,932	10,068	14
15	65,103	41,662	4,764	11
Executive	71,796	9,181	845	9

SOURCE: U.S. Office of Personnel Management, Office of Workforce Information, Statistical Analysis and Services Division. Employment and Trends as of January 1989, Tables 1,2,3. Washington, D.C. (Percents by author)

* Average salary as of March, 1988. (Executive average computed by author from Grades 16,17,18) From Report to the Office of Management and Budget "Average Grade and Step Distribution",p.45.

The Law and Women

"A legal right is not something that someone gives you. It is something no one can take away."

Ramsay Clark, Former Attorney General
of the United States

Federal Law

EMPLOYMENT

Federal/State Employment Service; cooperative administration; offices in major cities

- Job referral and training (free)
- Unemployment Insurance (U.I.)

Information and complaints:

*   *   *

Bureau of Apprenticeship and training (B.A.T.)
Federal/State partnership under National Apprenticeship Act

Apprentice is paid while learning.

Information and complaints:
Bureau of Apprenticeship and Training, Dept. of Labor, State Labor Department
Washington, D.C.

State Law

Most states have maximum of 26 weeks of U.I.
Benefits cannot be denied solely because of
pregnancy; but applicant must be seeking work,
and able and available for suitable job.

Nearest state employment office; contact manager.

*

State Apprenticeship Councils

78

Federal law | State law

MINIMUM WAGE/MAXIMUM HOURS

Fair Labor Standards Act (FLSA)

- Federal minimum: $3.80/hr (1990)
- Overtime after 40 hours
- Covers workers producing goods and services sold in interstate commerce; administrative and executive positions not covered.

Information and complaints: Nearest office, Wage & Hour Employment Standards Administration, U.S.Dept. of Labor
* * * * * * * * * * * * * * * * * * * *

Equal Pay Act (1963)

Amended FLSA to require equal pay for men and women workers doing essentially similar work in the same establishment.

Information and complaints: Nearest office, Wage & Hour

Laws and dollar minimum varies by state All but 9 states have statutory minimum; some are higher than federal.

Covers local service industries

State labor department

WORKING CONDITIONS

Occupational Safety and Health Act (OSHA) 1970

Employers are required to provide workplaces free of hazards that may harm workers (unsafe storage; toxic substances) and must provide safety equipment if needed.

Information and complaints: Nearest OSHA office

Some cities and states have laws requiring that employees be informed of toxic substances or similar hazards.

City or state labor department

Federal law	State Law

JOB DISCRIMINATION

Federal law

Equal Employment Opportunity Commission (E.E.O.C.)
Enforces Title VII of 1964 Civil Rights Act

Forbids discrimination by employers with 15 or more employees; by unions with 15 or more members; by employment agencies - in referrals; hiring; training; promotion,or other conditions of employment; forbids sexual harassment.

Information and complaints: U.S. EEOC, 1400 "L" St.,NW, Suite 200, Washington, D.C. 20005 or nearest office - large cities.

Executive Order #11246,#11375

Forbids discrimination by employers holding federal contracts; requires contractors to take affirmative action in recruiting, hiring, promotion, and apprenticeship or other training programs.

Information and complaints: E.E.O.C.

Pregnancy Discrimination Amendment (1978)

Amends Title VII to require that employers with 15 or more employees, who offer medical, leave or other benefit programs must include pregnancy.

Information and complaints: E.E.O.C.

Age Discrimination in Employment(ADEA) (1967)

Forbids discrimination in employment for persons between age 40 and 70. Applies to all public employers; private employers of 20 or more; employment agencies serving covered employers and labor unions of more than 25 members.

Information and complaints: E.E.O.C.

State Law

Fair Employment Practice laws (in force in all but 6 states; many also have Civil or Human Rights Commissions.)

Written complaints must usually be filed with state agency before federal E.E.O.C. will act.

NOTE: Complaints must be filed within a certain time period, usually 6 months.

Federal law

RETIREMENT PENSIONS AND HEALTH BENEFITS

Employment Retirement Income Security Act (ERISA) 1974

Retirement programs must be filed with U.S. Department
of labor.(Parttime workers may be excluded)

U.S.Supreme Court ruled in 1978 that employer may not
charge women higher rates than men for participation
in a retirement plan; and ruled in 1983 that
employment-related pensions must be equal for similarly
situated men and women. (under C.R. Act, Title VII)

Comprehensive Omnibus Budget Reconciliation Act (COBRA) 1986

Requires employer to offer group health insurance coverage
to former employees and their dependents, and to the
divorced, or separated spouses (and dependents)
of present employees. (Period up to three years)

Information and complaints: U.S. Secretary of Labor,
Washington, D.C. 20210.

THE LAW AND WOMEN (cont.)

Federal law	State law

CREDIT

Equal Credit Opportunity Act (ECOA) 1974; 1976

Applies to all creditors who regularly extend credit - (banks, finance companies, department stores); may not discriminate on basis of sex, marital status, race, religion, national origin, age, or receipt of public assistance.

Forbids asking whether you are widowed or divorced; lender must include income from part-time employment, AFDC, Social Security, unemployment compensation in computing total income; lender must give specific reasons for denial of credit.

Information and complaints: Equal Credit Opportunity, Washington, D.C. 20580

Some states have laws banning discrimination in granting of credit.

State office of Human Rights

HOUSING

Fair Housing Act 1968; 1974
Amended Title VIII of Civil Rights Act 1968

Forbids discrimination by sex in sale or rental of most housing - by owners, real estate brokers, mortgage financing companies.

Information and complaints: Fair Housing
U.S. Department of Housing
and Urban Development
Washington, D.C. 20410

Some states or local areas also have fair housing laws

State or local housing departments

Federal law   State law

EDUCATION

Education Amendments of 1972 - Title IX

Forbids sex discrimination in admissions and employment
in public and private schools receiving federal funds.
Covers vocational schools and graduate institutions,
but excludes private undergraduate colleges.
Requires appropriate funding of male and female
sports activities. (Religious institutions exempt)

(Amended 1988 by Civil Rights Restoration Act)

Vocational Education Act 1976

Requires states to establish Sex Equity coordinator to
encourage female enrollment in traditionally male
occupational programs.

Information and complaints: U.S. Secretary of Education
                            Department of Health and
                                   Human Services
                                 Washington, D.C.

Other federal laws may be useful in reversing
discrimination in educational opportunity, with
the assistance of the U.S. Attorney General,
Washington, D.C.;

Equal Educational Opportunities Act, 1974
Title IV - 1964 Civil Rights Act

Some states also have laws
forbidding discrimination
in educational opportunity.

State Department of Education

Federal law

State law

CHILD CARE*

Title XX, Social Security Amendments

Federal funds are made available to states to provide day care facilities for welfare recipients and other low-income families.

Funds are generally inadequate to satisfy demand for child care services.

Information and complaints: Secretary of U.S. Department of Health and Human Services Washington, D.C.

Some states have appropriated funds to supplement federal allotments for purposes of child care.

Office for Children at State House.

* The 1988 Family Security Act, in addition to tightening procedures and enforcement of laws affecting fathers delinquent in child support payments, is expected to provide federal funds for more child care facilities. Given the federal budget deficit, the provision of adequate funds is questionable.

Federal law   State law

CHILD SUPPORT

Title IV-D, Social Security Act Amendments,1977

Required states to improve collection of child support
for families on welfare.

Parent Locator Service - 1982

To assist state enforcement measures, permitted use of
federal records to trace delinquent parents, and the
interception of federal income-tax refunds. (Initially for
families on welfare only.

1984 Child Support Enforcement Amendments
Extended the provisions of the 1982 law to cover non-welfare
families, with respect to federal records use in tracing
delinquent parents; and provided for mandatory wage attachments;
placing liens on property; and tax-refund interceptions.

1988 Family Security Act

Tightened enforcement provisions of the 1984 and earlier laws;
permitted phased-in payroll deductions (beginning 1990);
beginning in 1994, child support awards will provide for
payroll withholding, unless parents choose otherwise.
Stronger penalties on states include loss of federal funds.

1987

State-by-State Index of Women's Legal Rights

Highest score is 4; lowest is -2

	Equal Employment	Pay Equity	Child Support	Community Property	Insurance		Equal Employment	Pay Equity	Child Support	Community Property	Insurance
Alabama	0	0	2	0	-2	Montana	2	2	1	0	3
Alaska	2	2	4	0	-2	Nebraska	2	0	4	0	-2
Arizona	2	-2	2	2	-2	Nevada	2	0	1	2	-2
Arkansas	0	-2	4	4	-2	New Hampshire	2	0	4	0	-2
California	2	2	1	2	-2	New Jersey	2	2	4	0	-2
Colorado	2	0	2	0	-2	New Mexico	2	4	2	4	-2
Connecticut	2	4	2	0	-2	New York	2	4	4	0	-1
Delaware	2	-2	2	0	-2	North Carolina	2	0	4	3	1
District of Columbia	2	0	2	0	-1	North Dakota	2	0	2	0	-2
Florida	2	2	2	0	-2	Ohio	2	2	2	0	-2
Georgia	0	-2	4	0	-2	Oklahoma	2	2	4	0	-2
Hawaii	2	2	2	0	1	Oregon	2	2	4	0	-2
Idaho	2	4	1	4	-2	Pennsylvania	2	0	2	0	-2
Illinois	2	0	2	0	-2	Rhode Island	2	0	2	0	-2
Indiana	2	0	4	0	-2	South Carolina	2	0	1	0	-2
Iowa	2	4	4	0	-2	South Dakota	2	4	4	0	-2
Kansas	2	0	2	0	-2	Tennessee	2	0	4	0	-2
Kentucky	2	0	2	0	-2	Texas	2	0	1	2	-2
Louisiana	2	2	2	4	-2	Utah	2	0	4	0	-2
Maine	2	2	2	0	-2	Vermont	2	4	1	0	-2
Maryland	2	2	4	0	-2	Virginia	0	0	4	0	-2
Massachusetts	2	2	2	0	1	Washington	2	4	4	2	-2
Michigan	2	4	4	0	1	West Virginia	2	2	2	3	-2
Minnesota	2	4	4	0	-2	Wisconsin	2	4	1	3	-2
Mississippi	0	0	4	0	-2	Wyoming	2	2	1	0	-2

Major Research Universities, by State

Florida
 Public
  Florida State University
  University of Florida
 Private
  University of Miami
Georgia
 Public
  Georgia Institute of Technology
  University of Georgia
 Private
  Emory University, main campus
Hawaii
 Public
  University of Hawaii, main campus
Illinois
 Public
  University of Illinois, Urbana
 Private
  Illinois Institute of Technology
  Northwestern University
  University of Chicago
Indiana
 Public
  Purdue University, main campus
  Indiana University, Bloomington
Iowa
 Public
  Iowa State University of Science and Technology
  University of Iowa
Kansas
 Public
  Kansas State University of Agriculture
   and Applied Sciences
  University of Kansas
Kentucky
 Public
  University of Kentucky
Louisiana
 Public
  Louisiana State University, Baton Rouge

State and School

Alabama
 Public
  Auburn University, main campus
Arizona
 Public
  University of Arizona
Arkansas
 Public
  University of Arkansas, main campus
California
 Public
  University of California, Berkeley
  University of California, Davis
  University of California, Los Angeles
  University of California, San Diego
 Private
  California Institute of Technology
  Stanford University
  University of Southern California
Colorado
 Public
  Colorado State University
  University of Colorado, main campus
Connecticut
 Public
  University of Connecticut, main campus
 Private
  Yale University
District of Columbia
 Private
  Catholic University of America
  George Washington University

87

MAJOR RESEARCH UNIVERSITIES[*], By State (cont)

State and School	State and School
Maryland	**New York**
Public	Public
University of Maryland, main campus	State University of New York, Buffalo,
Private	main campus
Johns Hopkins University	Private
Massachusetts	Columbia University, main division
Public	Cornell University, main campus
University of Massachusetts, Amherst	New York University
Private	Syracuse University
Harvard University	University of Rochester
Massachusetts Institute of Technology	Yeshiva University
Boston University	**North Carolina**
Brandeis University	Public
Tufts University	North Carolina State University, Raleigh
Michigan	University of North Carolina, Chapel Hill
Public	Private
Michigan State University	Duke University
University of Michigan, main campus	**Ohio**
Wayne State University	Public
Minnesota	Ohio State University, main campus
Public	University of Cincinnati, main campus
University of Minnesota, Minneapolis-St. Paul	Private
Mississippi	Case Western Reserve University
Public	**Oklahoma**
Mississippi State University	Public
Missouri	Oklahoma State University, main campus
Public	University of Oklahoma, main campus
University of Missouri, Columbia	**Oregon**
Private	Public
Washington University	Oregon State University
Nebraska	University of Oregon, main campus
Public	**Pennsylvania**
University of Nebraska, main campus	Public
New Jersey	Temple University
Public	Pennsylvania State University, main campus
Rutgers University, New Brunswick	University of Pittsburgh, main campus
Private	Private
Princeton University	Carnegie-Mellon University
	University of Pennsylvania

88

State and School

Rhode Island
  Private
    Brown University
Tennessee
  Public
    University of Tennessee, Knoxville
  Private
    Vanderbilt University
Texas
  Public
    Texas Agricultural and Mechanical University
    University of Texas, Austin
  Private
    Rice University
Utah
  Public
    University of Utah

Virginia
  Public
    University of Virginia, main campus
    Virginia Polytechnic Institute and State
      University
Washington
  Public
    Washington State University
    University of Washington
West Virginia
  Public
    West Virginia University, main campus
Wisconsin
  Public
    University of Wisconsin, Madison

* SOURCE: Research universities are defined by the Carnegie
           Commission on Higher Education as those institutions
           among the 100 leading universities in federal
           support over a period of years who awarded at least
           50 Ph.D.s (or M.D.s) in 1969-70. (See B. Fitzpatrick,
           Women's Inferior Education: An Economic Analysis.
           Boston, Pemberton Publishers, 1983. Chapter 3; Appendix C.
           P.O. Box 441558, Somerville, MA 02144)

Useful agencies providing assistance to women

Center on Social Welfare Policy and Law
    1029 Vermont Avenue, N.W., Washington, D.C. 20005-3592

Chicana Rights Project
    28 Geary Street, 6th floor, San Francisco, CA 94108

Federally Employed Women
    National Press Building,Rm.481, Washington, D.C. 20045

NAACP Legal Defense and Education Fund
    10 Columbus Circle, New York, N.Y. 10019

National Coalition for Women and Girls in Education
    1818 R Street, N.W., Washington, D.C. 20009

National Association of Women Business Owners
    2000 P Street, N.W., Washington, D.C. 20036

National Organization for Women (N.O.W.)
    425 13th Street, N.W., Washington, D.C. 20004

N.O.W. Legal Defense and Education Fund
    132 W. 43rd Street, New York, N.Y. 10036

National Women's Political Caucus
    1411 K Street, N.W., Suite1110, Washington, D.C. 20005

Project on Equal Education Rights (PEER)
    1029 Vermont Avenue., N.W. Suite 800, Washington, D.C. 20005

Wider Opportunities for Women
    1511 K Street, N.W., Room 345, Washington, D.C. 20006

Women's Equity Action League (WEAL)
    805 15th Street, N.W., Suite 822, Washington, D.C. 20005

REPRESENTATION OF WOMEN IN APPRENTICESHIP
By state, 1972 1/

Total and Female Apprentices, by Trade or Craft,
in Selected States, 1972*

State/Trade or Craft	Number of Programs	Number of Apprentices	
		Total	Female
Arkansas	32	332	0
California	318	26,385	76
Automotive mechanic	10	630	1
Butcher-meat cutter	16	1,060	2
Carpenter	22	12,034	3
Painter	23	1,688	28
Plumber-pipe fitter	36	1,824	1
Printing pressman	10	174	6
Miscellaneous trades	11	724	6
Colorado	80	2,421	4
Machinist	5	31	1
Delaware	19	253	4
Florida	99	5,955	4
Carpenter	9	1,894	1
Plumber-pipe fitter	15	1,140	1
Printing pressman	3	22	2
Illinois	277	11,396	27
Bookbinder	4	116	4
Carpenter	16	1,818	1
Lithographer	3	1,688	14
Printing pressman	20	285	8
Kansas	22	448	0
Massachusetts	63	3,133	13
Carpenter	13	501	1
Printing pressman	8	173	12

(continued)

1/ Current data by state, by job title, not available in June 1990.
(California, Rhode Island, District of Columbia, Puerto Rico, Hawaii,
and Virgin Islands data not recorded.)

In 1989, of 263,023 registered apprentices reported, women were 7.2% of
total.

State/Trade or Craft	Number of Programs	Number of Apprentices	
		Total	Female
Michigan	704	9,305	12
Bricklayer	9	110	3
Printing pressman	5	168	1
Tool and die maker	119	1,219	1
Mississippi	45	814	2
Electrical worker	10	236	2
Nevada	35	845	4
New Jersey	183	2,838	19
Printing pressman	7	56	4
Miscellaneous trades	5	50	15
New York	210	9,619	34
Electrical worker	36	3,401	1
Printing pressman	12	372	1
Ohio	396	7,243	16
Electrical worker	72	2,019	1
Iron worker	12	352	2
Printing pressman	13	161	9
Tool and die maker	45	367	2
Oklahoma	26	780	1
Pennsylvania	253	5,950	81
Bookbinder	6	93	25
Printing pressman	23	310	52
South Carolina	28	285	1
Texas	126	5,691	10
Carpenter	17	1,275	2
Painter	3	128	1
Printing pressman	14	196	5
Vermont	10	140	0
Wyoming	13	277	0

*Separate trade or craft statistics are shown only for those trades in which females were reported.

Note: Reports are required from each joint labor-management apprenticeship committee subject to Title VII that has: five or more apprentices in its entire program; and at least one employer sponsoring the program who has 25 or more employees; and at least one union sponsoring the program that operates a hiring hall or has 25 or more members. (The numbers reported above represent about one-third of all registered apprentices in 1972.)

Source: Equal Employment Opportunity Commission, Apprenticeship Information Report EEO-2 (Washington, D.C., 1972).

Reduced Retirement Income for Dual-earner Families Relative to Traditional Families

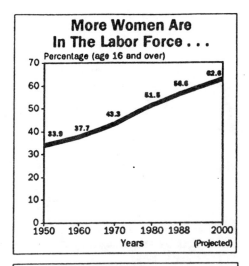

More Women Are In The Labor Force . . .

Percentage (age 16 and over)

(values shown: 33.9, 37.7, 43.3, 51.5, 56.6, 62.6 across years 1950, 1960, 1970, 1980, 1988, 2000)

Years   (Projected)

... But As Retired Families and Widows, They Will Be Worse Off

Avg. Annual Earnings	Dual Earner Family	Traditional Family
Husband	$17,500	$29,000
Wife	$11,500	$ 0
Total	$29,000	$29,000
1990 Soc. Sec. Monthly Benefit at Age 65		
Husband	$733	$ 975
Wife	$551	$ 487
Total	$1,284	$1,462
Survivor Benefit	$ 733	$975

Source: Bureau of Labor Statistics, 1985; Howard N. Fullerton, "New Labor Force Projections, Spanning 1988 to 2000," Monthly Labor Review (Nov. 1989)

Mother's Day Report 1990

SOURCE: Older Women's League. "Heading for Hardship: Retirement Income for American Women in the Next Century". 730 Eleventh Avenue, NW, Suite 300, Washington, D.C. 20001.

bibliographical references

In addition to sources listed after each chapter, the following readings are suggested:

American Association for the Advancement of Science. <u>Associations and Committees of and for Women in Science, Engineering, Mathematics and Medicine</u> Washington, D.C. , 1988. 1333 H Street, NW.

Bergmann, Barbara R. <u>The Economic Emergence of Women.</u> New York, 1986. Basic Books, Inc.

Burtless, Gary (ed) <u>A Future of Lousy Jobs? The changing structure of U.S. wages.</u> Washington, D.C. , 1990, Brookings Institution.

Crites, L. and Hepperle, W. <u>Women, the Courts, and Equality.</u> Newbury Park, CA 1987 Sage Publications.

DeCrow,K. <u>Sexist Justice</u>. New York. 1974, Random House.

Edelman, Marian Wright. <u>Families in Peril - An Agenda for Social Change.</u> Cam bridge,MA. 1987, Harvard University Press.

Ehrenreich, B. and English, D. <u>For her own good: 150 years of the experts advice to women. 1978,</u> Garden City, N.Y., Anchor Press.

Eisler, Riane. <u>Dissolution: Divorce, marriage and the future of women.</u> New York, 1977, McGraw Hill.

Ewen, Stuart. <u>Captains of Consciousness: Advertising and the social roots of the consumer culture.</u> New York, 1976. McGraw Hill.

FAIRTEST. <u>Standing Up to the SAT.</u> Cambridge, MA 1989, National Center for Fair and Open Testing, 342 Broadway.

Fuchs, Victor R. <u>How We Live: An Economic Perspective on Americans from Birth to Death.</u> Cambridge, MA. , 1983, Harvard University Press.

Galbraith, J.K. <u>Economics and the Public Purpose.</u> Boston, MA. , 1973, Houghton Mifflin. (Chapters 4 and 23)

Hoffman, Emily. <u>The Deserving and Non-Deserving Poor.</u> Department of Economics, Western Michigan University, 1984. (unpublished paper)

.Larwood, Laurie, etal (eds). <u>Women and Work.</u> Beverly Hills, CA, 1985, Sage Publications.

Leana, Frank. <u>Getting Into College.</u> New York, 1989, Hill and Wang

N.O.W. LDEF, <u>State by State Guide to Women's Legal Rights.</u> 99 Hudson Street. New York., 1987.

N.O.W. LDEF, Project on Equal Educational Rights. <u>Computer Equity Report: Sex Bias at the Computer Terminal: How Schools Program Girls</u>. Washington, D.C., 1413 K Street, NW, 1984.

Older Women's League. <u>Heading for Hardship: Retirement Income for American Women in the Next Century</u> Washington, D.C. 1990. 730 Eleventh Street NW,Suite 300.

Pottker, J. and Fishel, A. <u>Sex Bias in the Schools: The Research Evidence.</u> New Brunswick, NJ, Fairleigh Dickinson University, 1976.

R oss S. and Barcher, A. <u>The Rights of Women.</u> New York, 1983 (rev. edition) Bantam Books.

Simms, M.C. and Malveaux, J.M. (eds) <u>Slipping through the Cracks: The Status of Black Women.</u> New Brunswick, NJ. 1983 Transaction Books, Box C 24, Rutgers University.

Spain, Daphne. <u>Women's Demographic Past, Present, and Future.</u> Charlottesville,VA University of Virginia, Department of Sociology. (unpublished paper presented at Radcliffe Conference on Women in the 21st Century, 1989)

U.S. Commission on Civil Rights. <u>A Growing Crisis: Disadvantaged Women and their Children. (released April 11, 1983)</u>

U.S. Department of Labor. <u>Employment and Earnings</u> (monthly); <u>Monthly Labor Review (monthly) Occupational Outlook Handbook.Washington, D.C.</u>

U.S. Department of Labor. <u>A Working Woman's Guide to Her Job Rights (1988)</u>

U.S. Department of Labor. Women's Bureau. <u>A Woman's Guide to Apprenticeship.</u> (latest)

U..S.Social Security Administration. <u>A Woman's Guide to Social Security.(latest)</u>

Weitzman, L. <u>The Divorce Revolution.</u> New York:The Free Press, 1985.

index

About the author

Blanche Fitzpatrick is an economist specializing in labor economics, especially the problems of women in the labor market. She has been a Professor of Economics at Boston University since 1965, and has also taught at Goucher College in Maryland and at California State Universi at Fullerton. She has served on the Massachusetts Governor's Commission on the Status of Women, as a Trustee of the University of Lowell, and as a member of the Massachusetts Board of Higher Education. Her undergraduate work in economics was at Tufts University, followed by an M.A. from Stanford and the Ph.D. from Harvard. She has written articles and books on the problems of povert and unemployment.